AWESOME FACTS

29 USA
ROLL SINGER, 1935-1977
ELVIS PRESLEY

The Beatles
República
de Guinea Ecuatorial

United States

igloobooks

igloobooks

Published in 2013
by Igloo Books Ltd
Cottage Farm
Sywell
NN6 0BJ
www.igloobooks.com

SHE001 0713
2 4 6 8 10 9 7 5 3 1
ISBN 978-1-78197-589-3

Printed and manufactured in China

Contents

Introduction

In this book, you will embark on a **wonderful adventure**, discovering many new and exciting facts about the world in which you live. You can start by exploring outer space and learn how our Earth makes up a tiny part of the whole Universe. Then, go on to discover even more about our planet, its plant and animal kingdoms, our science and technology, and the world's different cultures.

Whether you read this book from start to finish, or simply dip into different sections that interest you, there is a wealth of fascinating information, as well as some awesome facts, just waiting to be discovered.

Interactive Instructions

On your mobile, or tablet device, download the **FREE** Layar App.

Look out for the **SCAN ME** logo and scan the whole page.

Unlock, discover and enjoy the enhanced content.

For more details, visit: **www.igloobooks.com**

Outer Space

1

THE UNIVERSE

Our planet has not always existed and the Earth is, in fact, a very young planet. Scientists believe the Universe to be around 14 billion years old, while the planet we live on in that Universe was only born around 4 billion years ago. And all of this began with an explosion called the Big Bang.

DID YOU KNOW?

The visible bang?

Astronomers are able to see the galaxies moving away from each other in many different directions as a result of the Big Bang.

AMAZING!

The Big Bang

The Universe was born as a result of what scientists now call the "Big Bang", which took place billions of years ago. In the beginning the whole Universe was squeezed inside a tiny bubble, which was thousands of times smaller than even the smallest pinhead. The bubble began to expand with unimaginable heat until it became so hot that it eventually exploded, allowing energy and matter – followed by atoms, gases and galaxies – to form. So, time, space, and matter all began with the Big Bang. In a fraction of a second, the Universe grew from something impossibly small to something that is bigger than a galaxy. It continues to grow even now and is expanding all the time.

Life begins

After studying ancient rocks scientists discovered that life, as we know it, started on Earth about 3,800 million years ago.

The birth of Earth

The young Earth was mainly made up of water with small pockets of dry land. Many scientists believe that life began in the lakes and oceans. The molecules in these lakes and oceans were mixed together, making them a bit like a vast "organic soup". It's thought that these molecules started to make copies of themselves and these new molecules then went on to become the first life on Earth.

DID YOU KNOW?

Amazing Universe Facts

1 THE SHUTTLE

NASA's Space Shuttle programme shut down in 2011 after over 30 years of space missions.

2 SPACE STATIONS

The International Space Station weighs more than 365,000kg (805,000lb) and has been occupied since 2000.

3 IS SPACE COLD?

Space itself doesn't have a temperature but the things in space do.

4 SAFE LANDING

In 2005 a Japanese spacecraft managed to land safely on an asteroid.

5 HOW FAR IS FAR?

The Universe is so vast that scientists measure distances in light years. A light year is the distance light travels in one year, which is about 8 trillion kilometres (5 trillion miles).

6 SHOOTING STARS

Shooting stars are meteors that heat up as they enter the Earth's atmosphere and several can be seen every hour each night.

The first star

Stars began to form 100 million years after the Big Bang. Clouds of hydrogen and helium gas clumped together, which began to exert huge gravity. This gravity pulled the atoms closer and closer together into the middle of the star. Having all of these atoms very close to each other resulted in the star sending out heat and light.

THE SOLAR SYSTEM

We live on Earth, which is part of our local Solar System, together with the Sun, the Moon and everything that is bound to us by gravity. Our Sun is just one star within The Milky Way galaxy, which is in turn just one galaxy within the entire Universe. The world we live in seems vast but is, in fact, a tiny part of a much larger Universe.

DID YOU KNOW?

The Oort Cloud

The Oort Cloud is a large group of icy objects that exists at the very edges of our Solar System. Scientists believe that it reaches out a distance of 7.4 trillion kilometres (4.6 trillion miles) from the Sun.

So far is it from our Sun's gravitational pull that passing stars can alter the orbit of objects in the cloud and then send them either into our Solar System or into interstellar space. The comet Hale-Bopp is thought to have come from the Oort Cloud.

Uranus 2,870 million kilometres (1,783 million miles) from the Sun

Neptune 4,500 million kilometres (2,800 million miles) from the Sun

Jupiter 778 million kilometres (483 million miles) from the Sun

Earth 150 million kilometres (93 million miles) from the Sun

Mercury 58 million kilometres (36 million miles) from the Sun

Saturn 1,430 million kilometres (890 million miles) from the Sun

Mars 228 million kilometres (142 million miles) from the Sun

The Sun

Venus 108 million kilometres (67 million miles) from the Sun

SUPER FACT!

The Asteroid Belt

The Asteroid Belt is in an area of space situated between the planets Jupiter and Mars. It is divided into two parts: the inner belt and the outer belt.

The inner belt, which is within 402 million kilometres (250 million miles) of the Sun, contains asteroids made from metals.

The outer belt, which lies 250 million miles beyond the Sun, consists of rocky asteroids. These appear darker than the inner-belt asteroids, and are rich in carbon. The asteroids can be tiny like a grain of sand or as much as 966km (600 miles) across.

The Kuiper Belt

This is a part of our Solar System but far, far beyond all the planets. It is similar to the Asteroid Belt, but around 20 times wider and 200 times larger. Like the Asteroid Belt, it's mainly made up of remnants from the formation of the Solar System.

INTERESTING!

The Milky Way

The Milky Way is the name of the galaxy that contains our Solar System. It is so-called because of its milky appearance. The Milky Way is spinning at a rate of 225km (140 miles) per second. In addition, the galaxy is travelling through space at the rate of 305km (190 miles) per second. This means that we are travelling at a total speed of 530km (330 miles) per second. It's hard to imagine, but within one minute you would be about 19,000km (11,800 miles) away from where you just were.

THE ROCKY PLANETS

Apart from the Sun, the largest members of the Solar System are the eight major planets. Nearest the Sun are four fairly small, rocky planets – Mercury, Venus, Earth and Mars. Beyond Mars is the Asteroid Belt, a region filled with rocky objects left over from the formation of the planets.

Mercury

Mercury is the nearest planet to the Sun. It speeds around the Sun once every 88 days. It is a small, rocky planet which is only about as wide as the Atlantic Ocean. Mercury could fit inside the Earth more than 18 times.

Mercury has no atmosphere and no water. At noon the temperature can reach as high as 450°C (842°F), but the nights are extremely cold, at -180°C (-292°F).

Venus

Venus is the second nearest planet to the Sun. It appears as a very bright morning or evening "star" which can be seen from the Earth. It is the brightest object in the night sky apart from the moon.

Venus is roughly the same size as Earth and is made up of the same rocky materials. However, it has a blanket of carbon dioxide around it, which is the same gas that humans breathe out. This blanket makes the planet even hotter than Mercury.

INTERESTING!

Earth

Earth is the third planet from the Sun. It takes the Earth 365 days (or one year) to complete an orbit of the Sun. The tilt of the axis that joins the North and South Poles means that the Earth has different seasons. When the North Pole points towards the Sun, then the northern countries have a summer. When the North Pole points away from the Sun, then winter starts in these countries. The seasons are the exact opposite to the south of the Equator.

The Moon

Venus

Mars

Mars is often referred to as the "Red Planet" because it appears in the sky as a reddish-coloured star. The planet's appearance is due to rust in the Martian rocks.

Mars is the fourth planet from the Sun and is the most earth-like of all the planets. However, days on Mars are slightly longer and it is also very cold; the average temperature is -63°C (-81°F), which is similar to winters in Antarctica.

The air on Mars is 100 times thinner than on Earth and is mostly made up of carbon dioxide. This means that visitors would need to wear oxygen masks the whole time in order to breathe.

Mars has canyons like the Earth's Grand Canyon. However, they are at least four times larger.

Awesome Planet Facts

1 JOURNEY TO MARS

Both the United States and the European Space Agency have announced that they plan to send men to Mars within the next 30 years.

2 PRECIOUS WATER

Earth is the only planet we know of with liquid water.

3 BLUE SUNSET

The sunset on Mars appears blue.

4 VENUS VISIT

The first spacecraft to visit Venus was called Mariner 2. The flight took place in 1962.

5 LIFELESS MERCURY

The surface of Mercury is covered with craters and completely dry. There is no possibility of life on Mercury.

6 LOOK UP TO THE SKY

Mercury is one of five planets that can be seen from Earth without using a telescope.

THE GAS PLANETS

On the far side of the Asteroid Belt are the four gas giants: Jupiter, Saturn, Uranus and Neptune. These planets are much bigger than the Earth, but very lightweight for their size. They are mostly made up of the gases hydrogen and helium. Even further out, there are the dwarf planets – Pluto and Eris – as well as the Kuiper Belt objects and comets.

Jupiter

Jupiter is the fifth and largest planet in the Solar System. Earth would fit inside Jupiter at least 1,300 times. Its diameter is 142,984km (88,846 miles). Even though it appears solid, it actually has no surface, but is a giant ball of gas.

The Great Red Spot, a storm several times bigger than the Earth, has been blowing non-stop on Jupiter for over 300 years and can be seen through a telescope.

Jupiter has the strongest gravitational pull of all the planets, making it the vacuum cleaner of the Solar System. It sucks in comets, asteroids and meteorites that could otherwise be on a collision course with Earth.

Uranus

Uranus is the seventh planet from the Sun and the third largest in size. The average temperature is -214°C (-353°F). One day on Uranus lasts just 17 hours and 14 minutes. Winters and summers at Uranus's Poles last for 21 years. Uranus is the only planet that orbits the Sun on its side.

Neptune

Neptune is the eighth planet from the Sun and is almost an identical twin of Uranus. One year on Neptune lasts for almost 165 Earth years. Neptune has 13 known moons, with Triton being the largest. Triton is very cold and covered in active ice volcanoes, which spurt out plumes of gas and dust.

SUPER FACT!

Saturn

Saturn is the sixth largest planet and before telescopes were invented, it was thought to be the planet furthest away from the Sun. Saturn weighs 95 times as much as our Earth. If you imagine putting all the planets in a big bowl of water, then Saturn is the only planet that would float.

Saturn is most well known for its rings. These magnificent rings are 273,300km (169,800 miles) wide and extremely thin, estimated to be less than a kilometre thick. The rings are split into categories: **Ring A, Ring B, Ring C, Ring D, Ring E, Ring F** and **Ring G**, totalling seven in all.

Saturn's rings are not as solid as they would appear and are, in fact, made up of particles of ice, dust and rock.

DiD YOU KNOW?

More Awesome Planet Facts

1 HOW MUCH DO YOU WEIGH ON JUPITER?

If you travelled to Jupiter on holiday, you would bae very heavy. If you weigh 32kg (70lb) on Earth, on Jupiter you would weigh 84kg (185lb). This is because Jupiter is such a large planet and so has more gravity.

2 URANUS'S RINGS

Uranus also has rings, though they don't stretch out as far as the rings of Saturn. The rings of Uranus are made up of black dust particles and large rocks.

3 STORMY WEATHER

Neptune suffers the most violent weather in our Solar System.

AMAZING!

Dwarf planets

Until very recently the furthest known planet was an icy, uninhabitable world called Pluto. In 2005 a planet called Eris was discovered. Eris is an icy planet that is at least as big as Pluto, but even further away from the Sun. However, in 2006 the International Astronomical Union decided that Pluto and Eris must be classed as "dwarf planets".

THE SUN

The Sun is at the very centre of our Solar System and is our nearest star, providing us with life-giving light and heat. Without the Sun our Earth would have been a dark and icy planet with no water and no life.

One year

The time it takes a planet to revolve around the Sun is called a year. The length of a year varies with the different planets. For example, an Earth year is 365 days long. Neptune has the longest year of all the planets, with one year lasting 60,190 Earth days.

Killer energy

Just a pinhead of the Sun's energy is enough to kill a person at a distance of 160km (100 miles).

SUPER FACT!

Great ball of fire

The Sun is a huge ball of super-hot gas, made almost entirely of hydrogen and helium. It is 1.4 million kilometres (870,000 miles) across, which is as large as 109 Earths lined up next to each other, and weighs 2 million trillion trillion trillion kilograms. That's the same as 330,000 Earths. In total, 1.3 million Earths would fit inside the Sun.

Hot, hot, hot!

The temperature on the surface of the Sun is about 5,500°C (9,932°F), which is more than 20 times hotter than an oven on maximum power. The temperature at the centre of the Sun is even hotter – at just over 15 million degrees Celsius (27 million degrees Fahrenheit)!

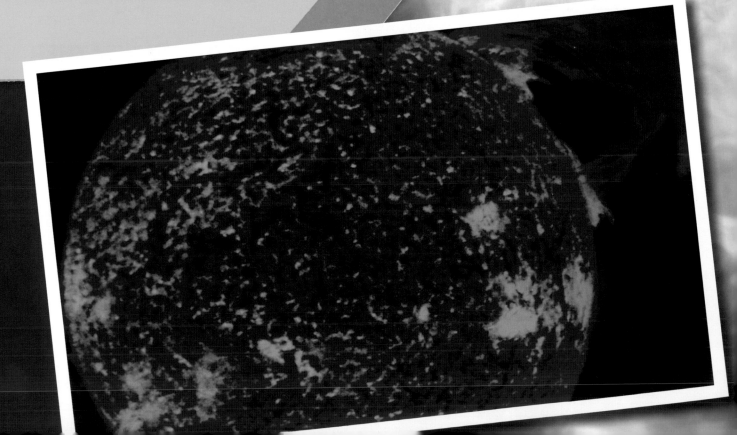

Solar eclipses

A solar eclipse is when the Moon passes between the Earth and the Sun, with most eclipses being only partial. A full solar eclipse will show a dark circle (the Moon) move in front of the Sun, with a ring of light (the corona) around it. The sky goes black, stars appear, and birds and animals go quiet, thinking that night-time has begun.

The speed of light

The Sun lies about 150 million kilometres (93 million miles) away from the Earth. Sunlight takes about eight minutes to reach us, travelling at an amazing speed of 300,000km (186,411 miles) per second.

A day on earth

The Earth takes one day (24 hours) to turn around its axis. When the part of the Earth you are on is facing the Sun, then it is day-time where you are.

Our Sun is dying

The Sun is about 4.5 billion years old and will begin to die in about 5 billion years. It will grow bigger and hotter, becoming a red giant star. Its heat will evaporate all the water on Earth, making our planet a hot, dry place – it will, in fact, become impossible for life to exist.

Eventually, the outer layers of the Sun will drift into space, making it shrink and cool. The Sun won't be much larger than the Earth, although it will still be quite hot; it will now be known as a white dwarf star. Once this white star has lost all of its heat, it will become a cold, dark black dwarf or dead star.

THE MOON

Our Moon has been circling Earth for over 4 billion years. Scientists think that it was once a part of Earth and call it "Earth's Child". When a planet crashed into the Earth, huge amounts of material were thrown into space and "captured" by the Earth's gravity before coming together to form the Moon. The "Big Splash" theory explains why rocks on the Moon and Earth are so similar.

Jupiter's moons

Jupiter has at least 66 moons or moonlets, making it the planet in our Solar System with the most known moons. It also has a faint ring system of small rocks and dust.

Jupiter also has the biggest moon in our Solar System. With a diameter of 5,268km (3,273 miles), this moon is even bigger than the planet Mercury.

Moon dust

The surface of the Moon is covered with a fine layer of dust beneath which lies a layer of crust.

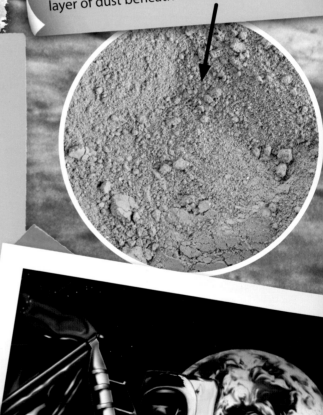

Lunar eclipse

A lunar eclipse is when the Earth stands exactly between the Sun and the Moon, making the Moon look dark orange. This happens up to three times a year.

AMAZING!

"That's one small step for a man, one giant leap for mankind."

The first person to set foot on the Moon was Neil Armstrong during the Apollo 11 space mission, which landed on the Moon on 20 July 1969.

Compass failure

There is no magnetic field on the Moon because of its small, solid, iron centre. Therefore, it is impossible for explorers to use a compass on the Moon.

SCAN ME
Instructions on page 5

Footprint

Although the Moon does not have as much gravity as the Earth, it does have some. If the Moon had no gravity, then explorers landing on the surface would not be able to leave behind footprints or flags – these would simply float away.

SUPER FACT!

Moon phases

The Moon's phases depend on how much and which side of it you see. It is a Full Moon when you can see all of the Moon's day-side. A Crescent Moon is when you can see only a thin curved part of the day-side. Sometimes you can't see the Moon at all because you're looking at its night-side. This is a New Moon. A lunar month lasts 29.53 days, which is the time from one Full Moon to another.

DiD YOU KNOW?

Amazing Moon Facts

1 ROUND AND ROUND

The Moon orbits the Earth once every 27.3 days.

2 MAKING WAVES

The Earth's tides are largely caused by the strong gravitational pull of the Moon.

3 SO NEAR, YET SO FAR

The average distance from the Moon to the Earth is 384,403km (238,857 miles).

4 CRATER SCARS

The surface of the Moon is covered with lots of craters due to violent collisions with comets and asteroids. Because the Moon doesn't have any atmosphere or weather, these craters remain well preserved.

5 SO HOT AND COLD

The Moon is very hot during the day, reaching a temperature of 107°C (225°F), but the nights are extremely cold at -153°C (-243°F).

SHINING STARS

You may think that stars are just little lights in the sky, but they are, in fact, huge balls of gas in outer space. They are made of hydrogen, helium and other elements. About 90 per cent of the lives of stars are spent fusing hydrogen to create helium. Stars produce light and heat. The twinkling stars you see in the night sky are actually very far away from Earth. Just like people, stars are born, grow old and die.

The birth of stars

When clumps of gas in space are drawn together by their own gravity and the middle of the clump is squeezed so hard that the temperature reaches 10 million degrees Celsius (18 million degrees Fahrenheit), a nuclear fusion reaction starts. This reaction is the birth of a star and the heat generated makes the star shine. The place where stars are born is known as a nebulae.

SUPER FACT!

Supernova – a death explosion

Stars end their lives in different ways. Most stars cool down to become white dwarfs and eventually fade into space to become black dwarfs. Some stars explode at the end of their life. This event is called a supernova.

Our Sun is a star!

The Sun is also a star, but is much closer to Earth – that's why it looks like a huge glowing ball.

Awesome Star Facts

Shooting stars

Shooting stars are not real stars. As sand-sized grains of dust, known as meteors, slam into the thin air above the Earth, they get really hot very quickly. The meteors burn up and leave bright streaks of light across the sky. This phenomenon is called "falling star" or "shooting star".

AWESOME FACT!

Pinpoints in the sky

Astronomers believe there are around septillion stars in the Universe. Our galaxy, The Milky Way, contains over 100 billion stars. The stars are so far away we can only see them as pinpoints of light in the sky. On a bright night, you can see about 3,000 stars with the naked eye.

The closest star to Earth, apart from the Sun, is Proxima Centauri, which is more than 40 trillion kilometres (25 trillion miles) away.

1 HOTTEST AND COLDEST

The surface of the coolest stars is below 3,500°C (6,332°F), while that of the hottest, brightest stars is over 40,000°C (72,032°F).

2 ORION NEBULAE

The closest nebulae to Earth is the Orion nebulae, which is 1,500 light years away.

3 WHY DO STARS TWINKLE?

Stars twinkle because the Earth's atmosphere is never still and the starlight twinkles as the air moves.

4 HOW HEAVY?

The heavier the star, then the shorter its life-span. Massive stars live for only a few million years, but lighter stars can live for trillions of years.

5 HOW OLD?

The oldest star discovered so far is the HE 1523-0901, which is estimated to be about 13.2 billion years old.

6 A STORM OF STARS

In 1966 the Leonid meteor shower produced 40 shooting stars every second!

SPACE PHENOMENA

Our Solar System not only contains the Sun, the eight major planets and their 240 known moons, but also phenomena such as dwarf planets, Kuiper Belt objects, asteroids, comets, meteoroids and space dust. All of these "objects" are held in orbit around the Sun by the pull of its gravity. At the centre of our Milky Way galaxy there is also a huge black hole, which is as big as 3 million suns. Don't worry… it's over 30,000 light years away!

AMAZING!

Big black holes

These are one of the most powerful and mysterious forces in the Universe. A black hole is an area in space where gravity has become so strong that nothing around it can escape – not even light!

Black holes are formed after a star goes supernova. The star will shrink to a single tiny point of infinite density called "singularity". The singularity sucks space into the black hole.

Black holes are truly invisible because they don't reflect any light. Scientists only know they exist because they can see light and objects around the hole.

Cool comets

Comets are balls of dirty ice that circle the outer Solar System. Occasionally, a comet is drawn towards our Sun. We may see a comet's tail, which is a mixture of materials such as gases, dust and rocks, in the night sky as the comet's surface is blown away by solar winds. The tail could be millions of miles long.

Encke's comet

The comet Encke is a periodic comet. This means it orbits the Sun on a regular basis – in this case every three years. It's famous for having the shortest orbit of any known comet.

Longest comet tail

The tail of the Great Comet, which passed by Earth in 1843, was more than 800 million kilometres (500 million miles) long. That is about the same as the distance from the Sun to Jupiter.

Mesmerising meteorites

Every day about 50 tonnes of rocky material from outer space lands on Earth. These rocks are called meteorites. Most of them come from the main Asteroid Belt between Jupiter and Mars, but it's been proven that some come from the Moon or Mars. By studying these rocks, scientists have learned a lot about the age and birth of our Solar System.

The largest meteorite

The largest meteorite on Earth is the Hoba West, which remains where it fell in Namibia, south-west Africa. When it was found in 1920, it measured 10m (33ft) across and weighed 66 tonnes.

Amazing asteroids

Asteroids are the thousands of rocky objects that orbit the Sun in a big band between the planets Jupiter and Mars. Meteoroids are often bits of broken-off asteroid.

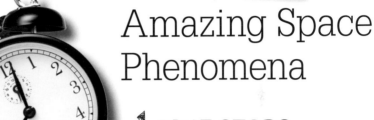

Amazing Space Phenomena

1 TIME STOPS

Scientists believe that time stands still inside a black hole!

2 THAT WAS CLOSE!

About every 50 million years a meteorite more than 10km (6 miles) in diameter hits the Earth.

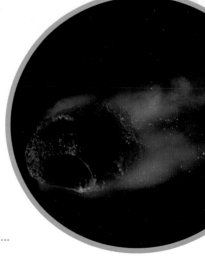

3 SUN WORSHIPPER?

The tail of a comet always points away from the Sun.

4 WHAT'S IN A NAME?

Before a meteorite hits the Earth, it's called a meteoroid. Most meteoroids burn up.

The Great Wall

The biggest known structure in the Universe is the Great Wall. This is a great sheet of galaxies, 500 million light years long and 16 million light years thick.

SPACE EXPLORATION

Humans have been able to travel in space for about 50 years. In that time more than 100 robotic craft have explored space, revealing more about the planets, moons, asteroids and comets. They fly by, orbit or land on these other worlds. As well as humans, animals such as dogs, monkeys and rats have all been sent into space to help with research.

People in space

Since 1961 more than 450 people have travelled into space. So far, mankind has only landed on the Moon, but we are planning to set foot on Mars in the near future.

AMAZING!

First animals in space

Fruit flies were the first creatures to be launched into space – and survive – on board the V-2 rocket on 20 February 1947. However, the first mammal to orbit the Earth was a Russian dog called Laika. Sadly, she died because the technology to return her from orbit hadn't yet been developed.

Belka and Strelka

On 19 August 1960 Sputnik 5 was the first spacecraft to carry animals into orbit and return them alive. On board were the dogs Belka and Strelka.

First man and woman in space

Russian Yuri Gagarin was the first human in space. His trip in April 1961 took him once round the Earth and lasted for 108 minutes.

Valentina Tereshkova was the first woman to fly into space. She made a three-day journey aboard Vostok 6 in June 1963.

AWESOME FACT!

Moon walker

Neil Armstrong was the first person to set foot on the Moon. He spent two hours and 35 minutes there. His footsteps will remain forever as the Moon doesn't have any weather to wash them away.

Space tourism

On the 28 April 2001 American millionaire Dennis Tito became the first space tourist when he paid around 20 million dollars for a ride in a Russian Soyuz spacecraft. Dennis spent a week in orbit, spending most of his time visiting the International Space Station. He had to train for 900 hours just to be a passenger!

Space shuttles

The space shuttle programme, run by NASA from the Kennedy Space Centre in Florida in the United States, was a revolutionary moment in the history of space travel as it allowed spacecraft to return to Earth and be used again for another flight, rather like an aeroplane. The first test flight took place in 1981. The space shuttles Enterprise, Columbia, Challenger, Discovery, Atlantis and Endeavour were used a total of 135 times from 1981 to 2011.

SCAN ME
Instructions on page 5

DID YOU KNOW?

Cool Space Facts

1 FLY THE FLAG!

There are six American flags planted on the Moon.

2 FAR, FAR AWAY

The Voyager 1 spacecraft left Earth in 1977 and is now the most distant human-made object in space.

Planet Earth

2

EARTH FACTS

About 4.5 billion years ago, a mass of rocky, iron-rich material, the beginnings of Planet Earth, was orbiting a young star – our Sun. Meteorites smashed into the young planet and welded together. This process generated so much energy that the whole planet melted, with the heavy iron sinking to the centre to become the Earth's Core. Lighter rocks then formed the Mantle and the Crust. This was the birth of Planet Earth. Our planet is very special since it's the only planet in our Universe on which life is known to exist.

1. The Inner Core

The Earth's Inner Core has a diameter of 2,400km (1,500 miles) and is made up of iron and nickel. Although the Inner Core is extremely hot, it is so deep within the Earth and under so much pressure that it remains solid. With temperatures of 5,000°C (9,032°F), it is about as hot as the surface of the Sun.

2. The Outer Core

The Outer Core is also made from iron and nickel. The only difference between the Inner and Outer Cores is that the Outer Core is liquid. It is this liquid metal swirling around the solid core of the Earth that creates our magnetic field. This layer is about 2,300km (1,400 miles) thick.

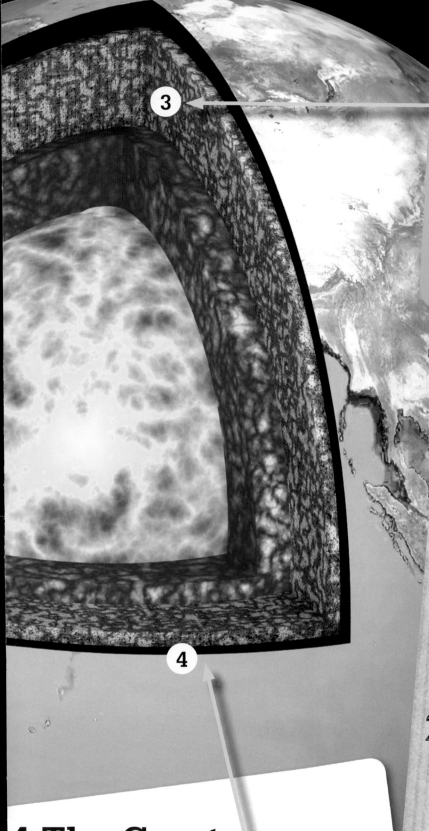

3

3. The Mantle

The next layer is the Mantle, which is about 3,000km (1,864 miles) deep. Many people think of this as lava, but it is actually made from rock. However, the rock is so hot that it flows under pressure and creates a slow-moving current as hot rock rises from the depths and cooler rock descends. The Mantle is divided into the upper mantle and the lower mantle.

4

4. The Crust

The last layer is the Crust, which is about 8km (5 miles) thick under the oceans and an average of 40km (25 miles) thick beneath the continents. These areas are known as oceanic and continental crust, respectively. The currents within the Mantle broke the Crust into blocks (or plates), which move around slowly.

DID YOU KNOW?

Awesome Earth Facts

1 AN EARTH YEAR

The Earth orbits the Sun once every 365.24 days. Our calendar has 365 days, so we need to add an extra day in February every four years in order to make up the time we haven't counted. We call a year with an extra day a "leap year".

2 CLEVER COPERNICUS

In the 1500s most people thought the Earth was at the centre of the Universe. A Polish astronomer called Copernicus was the first to suggest that the Earth was, in fact, orbiting the Sun.

3 FLAT OR ROUND?

People used to think the Earth was flat and that you could fall off the end! In the 6th century BC, Pythagoras, a Greek mathematician, was one of the first people to work out that the Earth was spherical.

THE EARTH'S ATMOSPHERE

Just as the Earth is split into different layers, including the Core and the Mantle, so too is the atmosphere. Not only does the atmosphere give us air to breathe, but it also protects us from meteorites and radiation. Our atmosphere has five distinct layers.

The Troposphere

The first layer of the atmosphere is called the Troposphere. It is only 17km (11 miles) high and provides us with the air we breathe and most of our weather. The higher you go in the Troposphere, the colder it gets.

The Stratosphere

The Stratosphere is the next layer. It reaches about 48km (30 miles) above Earth and includes the ozone layer. It is warmer than the Troposphere, as the ozone layer blocks the ultraviolet rays of the Sun and absorbs their energy. The temperature near the Troposphere is -80°C (-112°F), but at the top the temperature rises to almost 0°C (32°F).

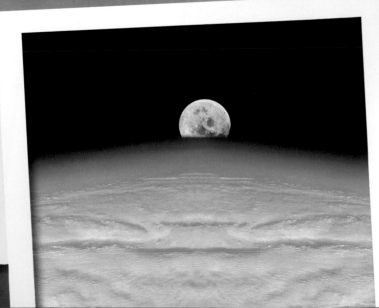

The Mesosphere

This layer is colder than the Stratosphere with temperatures going down to nearly -120°C (-184°F). Meteoroids generally burn up in this layer, which stretches about 85km (53 miles) above the Earth.

The Ionosphere

The next layer is the Ionosphere, which extends about 690km (430 miles) above Earth. The Ionosphere is so thick that most scientists consider it to be a part of outer space. The International Space Station and many satellites orbit within the Ionosphere. This layer has a lot of electrical energy and is responsible for the Northern and Southern lights.

The Exosphere

Beyond the Ionosphere lies the Exosphere. This is the layer between the Ionosphere and the solar storms. When the Sun is quiet, the Exosphere can extend further outwards by up to 10,000km (6,214 miles), where it merges with outer space.

DID YOU KNOW?

Atmospheric Facts

1 HOW THICK?

The Earth's atmosphere reaches a total of 690km (430 miles) above Earth.

2 LIFE ON EARTH

Our Earth is the only planet that has liquid water on its surface and oxygen in the atmosphere, conditions that make it possible for life to exist.

THE EARTH'S CRUST

Soon after the Earth was formed billions of years ago, its rocky outer crust solidified. The Earth's Crust may look like a solid layer of rock but it is, in fact, a brittle shell that is floating on the deeper-laying Mantle of partly molten rock. Movements in the Mantle have made the crust crack into separate plates. These plates are constantly being pulled apart and pushed together.

THE EARTH'S TECTONIC PLATES

Floating continents

There are about 15 larger tectonic plates and almost 40 smaller ones. Together they form the ocean floors and some of the larger ones carry the continents. The plates carrying the continents are made of a thicker, but lighter, rock that makes them float on the Earth's Mantle.

DID YOU KNOW?

Earth's biggest tectonic plate

The Pacific Plate, which forms the floor of the Pacific Ocean, has an area of nearly 103 million square kilometres (40 million square miles), making it the biggest tectonic plate on Earth.

Dramatic change

The Earth's plates move very slowly by an average of ~7cm (1½–3in) a year. This may seem slow, but the movement has changed the appearance of the Earth dramatically over billions of years.

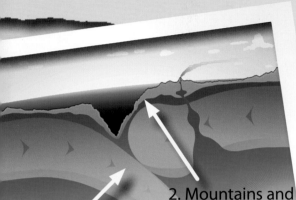

1. Oceanic plate slides under a continental plate.

2. Mountains and volcanoes may be pushed up.

Growing mountains

Occasionally an oceanic plate slides under a continental plate. When this happens mountain ranges may be pushed up. Sometimes the movement even creates a volcano. Some mountains are continuing to rise by 5mm (⅕ in) a year in places.

Changing oceans

The oceanic parts of the tectonic plates are constantly changing shape, making the oceans smaller or bigger. Although the plates carrying the continents move, they don't change shape.

AMAZING!

Moving continents

The Earth's continents all lie on different plates. The movement of these plates makes the continents move around the planet, too. This is called "continental drift". About 200 million years ago, there was only one big continent, called Pangaea, which was surrounded by one huge ocean.

200 million years ago

100 million years ago

Now

WHEN THE PLATES CAUSE DISASTER

The movement of the Earth's tectonic plates and the shifting positions of the continents can cause natural disasters such as earthquakes and tsunamis – the overwhelming power of these phenomena can cause a great deal of devastation and lead to the loss of human life.

Earthquake alarm!

Fault lines occur where continents meet. At points along these fault lines, the pressure may increase beneath the surface, which can cause the plates to move suddenly. This makes the rocks nearby shake, so setting off an earthquake.

The San Andreas Fault

A well-known fault line lies in California in the United States. It is called the San Andreas Fault. Movements along this plate have caused major earthquakes in the cities of both San Francisco and Los Angeles.

Tsunamis

When an earthquake takes place on the seabed, it can trigger giant waves called tsunamis. Tsunamis travel through the water at speeds of up to 800 km/h (500 mph). As a tsunami approaches land, the water forms deadly waves many metres high.

DID YOU KNOW?

Amazing Earthquakes and Tsunamis

1 SAVED BY SCIENCE

In 1975 Chinese scientists correctly predicted an earthquake and saved the lives of many people.

2 TALLEST TSUNAMI

The largest recorded tsunami was a wave measuring 524m (1,719ft) in Lituya Bay in Alaska.

3 BIGGEST EARTHQUAKE

In 1960, the world's biggest recorded earthquake took place in Chile. It had a magnitude of 9.5 and killed 1,655 people. The earthquake also triggered a tsunami that killed another 61 people in Hawaii, 138 in Japan and 32 in the Philippines.

4 EARTHQUAKES EVERYWHERE

Each year between 200 and 300 earthquakes are detected in the United Kingdom.

DID YOU KNOW?

Seismograph

It is not possible to predict earthquakes with absolute certainty, but, with the help of a seismograph, people can measure the movement of the plates and be more sure of when a possible earthquake may occur.

THE WORLD OF VOLCANOES

A volcano is a landform from which molten rock erupts through the Earth's surface. It usually takes the form of a mountain with most volcanoes sited near the edges of tectonic plates.

Volcano hot-spots

Most volcanoes occur along the fault lines of tectonic plates. Some volcanoes sit on so-called "hot-spots". These are weak spots in the Earth's Crust above areas of extreme heat in the Earth's Mantle. Hawaii was formed by the eruption of volcanoes on a hot-spot in the Pacific Plate.

SUPER FACT!

What's inside a volcano?

Crater The mouth of a volcano is called a crater. The crater is the circle of rocks around the volcano's main vent.

Main vent When an eruption takes place, magma rises up towards the surface through the volcano's main vent. Larger volcanoes will also have smaller secondary vents.

Magma chamber A large pool of molten rock, called magma, sits under the Earth's Crust in a magma chamber.

What happens when a volcano erupts?

The magma is lighter than the surrounding solid rock. So, it will rise up and collect in magma chambers. Sometimes the pressure builds up in these chambers so much that the magma rises even further than the chambers, thus escaping through vents into the crater of the volcano. Explosions are possible, but do not always occur.

SCAN ME
Instructions on page 5

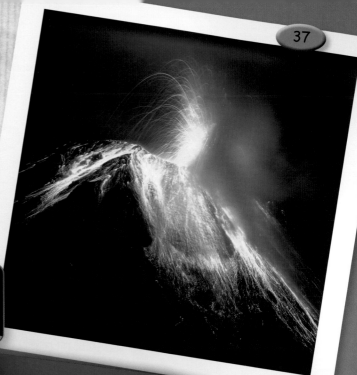

AMAZING!

Lava and magma

Magma is the molten rock that forms the Mantle layer of the Earth and is waiting in chambers deep down in the volcano. When magma erupts and reaches the surface of the Earth, we call it lava.

Explosion or no explosion?

When the magma is thin and runny, gases can escape easily and the magma – now known as lava – just flows out of the volcano. This rarely kills people because the flow is slow enough for people to get out of the way. It can destroy everything in its path, however, including buildings and trees.

But when the magma is thick and sticky, the gases cannot escape easily. Pressure builds up and the volcano is most likely to have an explosive eruption. Magma and ash will be blasted into the air. If the ash cloud is thick enough, then it can suffocate plants, animals and people.

Dormant volcanoes

Some volcanoes rarely erupt. When a volcano doesn't erupt, then we call it a dormant or sleeping volcano.

Extinct volcanoes

Volcanoes that haven't erupted in recorded history are said to be extinct. Scientists don't expect these volcanoes to erupt ever again.

THE WORLD'S BIOMES

The climate of a region determines what plants can grow and what animals will be able to survive there.

Desert

A desert is an area that gets very little rain, which means that not much plant growth is possible. The Sahara Desert is the world's largest desert. Temperatures regularly exceed 50°C (122°F) during the day, while at night it cools to freezing point.

Tropical grassland

In tropical areas that don't get much rain it's simply too hot for trees to grow, so these areas are full of grasses. They are often known as savannas.

Mountains

The mountain biome is a combination of other biomes. At the foot of the mountain you will find forests, first deciduous, then boreal forest. As you get higher up, it gets colder and more tundra-like with grasslands and shrubs. Finally, the mountain tops are bare rock and snow.

SUPER FACT!

Temperate grassland

Temperate areas in the middle of big continents only receive small amounts of rain. The rainfall is not enough for trees to grow, so grassy steppes and prairies develop instead.

Tropical rainforest

The plentiful sunshine and warm, heavy rain around the equator provide the perfect conditions for the dense plant growth of the tropical rainforests. About half of the animals in the world live in these forests.

Temperate forest

In temperate areas near the oceans, the temperature is not too hot and not too cold, allowing trees to grow very well in summer. In winter most of the trees stop growing and even lose their leaves.

Taiga forest

Towards the Arctic it is very cold. In the zone south of the tundra, where it is just warm enough for trees to grow, taiga (or boreal) forest has developed. The trees there have needle-like leaves and are well adapted to survive the long, freezing winters.

Mediterranean

The dry shrublands between the desert and the temperate zone are named after the Mediterranean area where these are most commonly found. The tough-leaved plants that live there can survive very hot summers.

AMAZING!

Polar and tundra

Temperatures are too low for trees to grow near the polar regions. Dominant plants on the tundra include grasses, mosses, lichens and shrubs.

A WORLD OF WEATHER

There are many different facets to the weather, including wind direction, wind force, precipitation, temperature, sunshine, visibility and the clouds. The area where you live and the air pressure there determines what kind of weather you will have.

The Water Cycle

All of the world's water has been on Earth for billions of years. The Earth and mankind are constantly using and re-using this water. We call this system the Water Cycle.

CONDENSATION

PRECIPITATION

EVAPORATION

COLLECTION

DID YOU KNOW?

Evaporation

The water in seas, oceans and rivers, as well as in puddles after a storm or the water in your glass, will all evaporate due to heat. When water evaporates it changes from a liquid to a gas (or water vapour) and then travels up into the atmosphere.

Condensation

Water vapour rises up and up into the atmosphere until it cools down and turns back into droplets of water. The process of turning back into water is called condensation. The water droplets then combine to form clouds in the sky.

Precipitation

Clouds contain thousands of these tiny water droplets. At first the droplets are too light and small to fall and so float in the air. But when millions of these droplets come together, they are finally heavy enough to fall as rain, snow, hail or sleet.

Collection

Once the water has fallen, it evaporates and starts the Water Cycle again. Before evaporating, however, it has to collect first. This happens in puddles, streams, rivers and seas. Water also becomes a part of the "ground water" and is used by plants.

Sleet, snow and hail

Although sleet and snow both happen when it is extremely cold, they are formed in different ways. When rain passes through a layer of cold air, the rain freezes and turns to sleet. Snow is formed when the water vapour doesn't condense in the air first, but turns into a solid phase at once and becomes snow.

Hail is mostly formed in a stormy atmosphere. The water droplets in a cloud freeze and the wind in the atmosphere blows them around, making more droplets join the ice pellets. When the ice pellets get too big and heavy, they fall as hail.

SUPER FACT!

Blow, wind, blow!

During the day the Sun heats the air above the land and areas of water such as oceans and lakes. The air above the land heats up faster than the air above the water. This uneven heating of the air is caused by different surfaces on the Earth, such as water, land, forests, rivers and deserts.

The air above areas of water is cooler and heavier, while the warmer air above land expands and rises. The cooler air then rushes from the water to the land to take the place of the warm air. This rush of air is called wind.

Awesome Weather Facts

1 ALL COLD AIR

Fresh snow is more than 90 per cent trapped air.

2 UNIQUE BEAUTY

No two snowflakes have the same shape, but they all have six sides.

3 RAIN, RAIN, RAIN

The most rainfall recorded in 24 hours is 182.5cm (72in) in La Reunion, near Madagascar. This was during tropical cyclone "Denise" on 8 January 1966. The most rainfall ever recorded in one year is 2,540cm (1,000in) in Cherrapunji, in India.

4 LET IT SNOW!

The highest snowfall ever recorded in a one-year period was 3,109cm (1,224in) in Mount Rainier, in the United States, from February 1971 to February 1972.

5 HEAVYWEIGHT HAIL

The heaviest hailstone ever recorded weighed 1kg (2¼ lb) and landed in Gopalganj District, Bangladesh, on 14 April 1986.

EXCITING WEATHER

The weather is one of our most popular topics of conversation. People moan about it a lot – it can be too wet, too windy, too hot or too cold! However, many people feel that weather events such as thunder and lightning or extremes of temperature are exciting, while phenomena like rainbows are beautiful.

INTERESTING!

Thunder and lightning

Hot air rises and cold air sinks. The cold air is constantly moving to replace the rising hot air, so creating wind. Sometimes, however, this can also cause thunder and lightning. A thunderstorm begins when wind picks up air containing a lot of water vapour. This happens when two blasts of wind run into each other or at places where a mountain pushes the air up.

The rising water vapour turns into droplets and this creates an electrical tension. This might be because the land is much hotter than the air temperature. When the tension gets too high, lightning strikes the Earth. The bolt of lightning heats the surrounding air until it's hotter than the surface of the Sun. This super-hot air then expands and pushes hard against the colder air next to it. This push causes the vibrations in the air that we hear as thunder. When the air runs out of water, the storm stops.

Rainbows

When the sun shines and it suddenly starts to rain too, one of Earth's most beautiful phenomena appears: a rainbow. Sunlight is made up of a spectrum of colours – red, orange, yellow, green, blue, indigo and violet – which together appear white. When sunlight passes through drops of rain, the drops "split" the light into the different colours. Interestingly, you can only see the colours when you are standing between the rain and the Sun and when the Sun is not too high in the sky.

It's all foggy

Fog is a cloud that occurs at ground level rather than in the sky. When the temperature of the air just above the land cools to the "dew point", it can't take up any more water vapour. After cooling even more, it loses its ability to hold all of that water vapour and forces some of it to condense, so forming droplets of water. All these droplets hanging just above the ground form fog.

Hot Equator

Sunlight shines on the Earth's surface at a smaller angle around the Equator than it does at any other place. This means that a ray of sunlight has to heat less of a surface area here than in, say, the United Kingdom, making it generally much warmer in equatorial countries.

DID YOU KNOW?

More Awesome Weather Facts

1 MOON RAINBOWS

Rainbows also appear on the Moon, but they are less clear than here on Earth because the Moon's light is only reflected sunlight.

2 TAKE COVER

You are safer in the ocean because nine out of ten lightning bolts strike the land rather than the oceans.

3 IT'S SO HOT!

Earth's highest recorded temperature of 58°C (136°F) was measured on 13 September 1922 in Al'Aziziyah, in Libya.

4 IT'S SO COLD!

The coldest temperature ever recorded on Earth was in Vostok Station, in Antarctica. It plummeted to -89.2°C (-128.56°F) on 21 July 1983.

5 WHAT A GALE

The fastest wind speed ever recorded was 372 km/h (231 mph) at Mount Washington, in the United States on 12 April 1934.

EXTREME WEATHER

The weather is usually predictable. Although the weather forecaster isn't always right about the weather, it's usually cloudy, sunny or rainy. However, our climate is changing as a result of global warming and the weather is changing, too – getting less predictable, more dangerous, and more extreme!

AMAZING!

SCAN ME
Instructions on page 5

Instructions on page 5

DID YOU KNOW?

Monstrous monsoons

Extreme weather such as a monsoon is quite predictable. Monsoons are rainstorms that last for weeks or months, and come back every year at regular times. Although predictable, they are no less damaging for that.

Terrible tornadoes

When rising hot air is very strong, it can develop into a swirling wind of clouds. This is known as a tornado or twister. When the tornado reaches the ground, it can cause a great deal of damage. Usually forming over land, tornadoes only last for a few minutes and rarely for more than a couple of hours.

Horrendous hurricanes

A hurricane is similar to a tornado – a damaging windstorm – but they are not exactly the same. Where a tornado is rarely wider than a mile, a hurricane can be miles wide. A hurricane always forms above warm ocean water and will last for days and sometimes even over a week. The high winds of a hurricane are always accompanied by heavy rain, which can cause flooding. Hurricanes are sometimes called cyclones or typhoons. They can also create tornadoes.

How hot is it?

We say we are having a heatwave when it is abnormally hot and unusually humid for a few days to over a week. This makes a precise definition difficult because what is considered abnormally hot differs throughout the world.

In Adelaide, Australia, a heatwave is defined as five consecutive days at or above 35°C (95°F) or three consecutive days at or over 40°C (104°F). In the Netherlands, a period of five consecutive days with temperatures of 25°C (77°F) and above is classified as a heatwave, as long as the temperature exceeds 30°C (86°F) for at least three of those days.

Driest places on Earth

Although Antarctica is freezing cold and full of snow and ice, it has never had any rain. Another extreme is the Atacama Desert in Chile – some places in this desert have had no rainfall for 400 years!

Extreme Weather Facts

1 TORNADO ALLEY

The United States has more tornadoes than any other country in the world, with an average of 1,200 a year, because it is located within "Tornado Alley".

2 DEADLY TORNADO

The worst tornado in history was the Daultipur-Salturia tornado in Bangladesh, which took place on 26 April 1989, killing around 1,300 people.

3 GO FASTER!

You can only outrun the fastest tornadoes by driving at 113 km/h (70 mph) in a car.

4 HURRICANE DEATH TOLL

Over the past 200 years hurricanes have killed about 2 million people worldwide.

5 THE EYE OF THE STORM

The weather in the "eye" or centre of a hurricane is usually calm, while the winds just outside the eye are the strongest.

FIRES AND FLOODS

As well as extremes of heat and cold, ferocious winds and violent storms, the weather can also cause environmental disasters such as forest fires because of high temperatures and low rainfall or, at the opposite extreme, flooding as a result of heavy rains.

Forest fires

A forest fire moves at a speed of up to 23 km/h (14 mph), consuming everything in its path, including trees, flowers, animals and houses. Some fires can destroy an entire town and some of its residents. Forest fires are also known as wild fires.

It only takes one spark...

Burning campfires and cigarettes can cause forest fires. However, lightning, hot winds or even the Sun can produce enough heat to spark a fire, too. Due to climate change, the Earth is getting hotter and drier, factors which both encourage fires to start and give them more fuel. Strong winds are also occurring more often, which can spread the fires quickly over land.

World's largest wild fire

The Black Friday Bushfire in Australia's Victoria State is the largest wild fire in recorded history. It occurred on 13 January 1939, burned 20,200 square kilometres (7,800 square miles) and killed 71 people. Ash from the fire fell in New Zealand, 3,219km (2,000 miles) to the east.

America's worst fire

The worst wild fire in America was The Great Peshtigo Fire in northern Wisconsin and Michigan during the week of 8–14 October 1871. It destroyed 930,800 hectares (2.3 million acres). Although campfires started the fire, the dry summer and warm autumn winds made the fire burn out of control. Fire tornadoes were seen and the fire became so hot that people taking refuge in rivers were boiled to death.

DID YOU KNOW?

Fearsome floods

Excessive rain, a ruptured dam, rapidly melting mountain ice, large storms or even a tsunami can cause floods. Most floods take hours or even days to develop, giving residents enough warning time to prepare or evacuate. Other floods develop very quickly and with no warning. These flash floods can be extremely dangerous.

Super water power

Moving water has an awesome destructive power. Bridges, houses and trees are no match for fast-moving water. Cars can be picked up and carried off, and the water may even drag dirt from under a building's foundation, causing it to crack and tumble down.

A land of floods

In the last hundred years floods in Bangladesh have killed more than 50,000 people and destroyed the homes of nearly 32 million. In 1998 alone floods killed 3,500 people and caused more than £1.5 billion (US$ 2.3 billion) of damage. The geography of Bangladesh is a key factor in its vulnerability to flooding. It has 250 rivers and is also the drainage point for the Himalayas.

MOUNTAINS

Mountains are landforms that rise above the surrounding terrain. They are formed by the movement of tectonic plates in the Earth's Crust and usually made from rocks and earth. If an elevation is higher than 600m (1,968ft), it is known as a mountain; less than 600m, it is only classified as a hill.

Mountains everywhere

Mountains exist on every continent and even beneath the oceans. Mountains cover one-fifth of the Earth's surface and occur in 75 per cent of the world's countries.

AWESOME FACT!

Fresh water source

More than half of the fresh water in the world originates in mountainous regions and all of the major rivers are fed from mountains.

World's highest mountain

The highest mountain measured from sea level is Mount Everest, being 8,850m (29,035ft) high. However, Mount Everest (as well as all the other Himalayan mountains) is still growing taller, at a rate of about 6cm (2¼ in) per year.

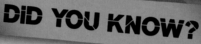

DID YOU KNOW?

World's tallest mountain

The tallest mountain in the world is called Mauna Kea. Measured from top to base, beneath sea level, it is 10,200m (33,465ft) tall. That is as big as about 1,020 buses in one big queue!

Mountain of ice

Glaciers are basically huge masses or mountains that are made completely from ice. Most glaciers are found at the Poles and cover about 15.5 million square kilometres (6 million square miles), but they are melting rapidly.

Mountain range

A mountain range is a group or chain of mountains that are close together. The Himalayas is the highest mountain range, with Mount Everest being its highest peak.

The Andes Mountain range in South America is the longest in the world. It stretches 7,200km (4,500 miles) from north to south, along the west coast of the continent. To walk from one side to the other would take you about 60 days!

Timberline

As you climb up a mountain, it gets colder and the vegetation changes. The foothills may be covered with broad-leaved forests. These change to needle-leaf trees on the upper slopes.

The timberline is an imaginary line on the mountain from which point it is too cold for trees to grow. You may still find grasses and some flowers growing. The peaks of the highest mountains are bare rock and often covered in snow.

OCEANS AND SEAS

Oceans cover about 70 per cent of the surface of the Earth and contain roughly 97 per cent of its water supply. The Earth's oceans are unique in our Solar System as no other planet has life-giving liquid water. In fact, life on Earth originated in the seas and oceans. The oceans have a huge influence on climate and weather. There are also many seas, often partly enclosed by land, which are smaller branches of the oceans.

AWESOME FACT!

The Southern Ocean

Until 2000 there were only four recognised oceans: the Pacific, Atlantic, Indian and Arctic Oceans. In the spring of 2000 the International Hydrographic Organisation named a new ocean: the Southern Ocean, which surrounds Antarctica.

The power of tides

Tides are caused by the rotation of the Earth and the gravitational pull of the Moon and Sun on the water in the seas and oceans.

Wind and waves

Waves are formed by wind blowing on the surface of an ocean or sea. Waves seem to move horizontally, but are actually moving up and down.

The biggest recorded wave, which reached a height of 524m (1,720ft), was caused by an earthquake and appeared in Lituya Bay on the southern coast of Alaska in 1958.

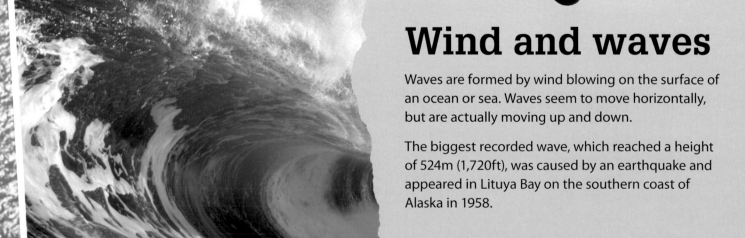

A Pacific giant

The largest ocean on Earth is the Pacific Ocean, which means "peaceful sea", although it is surrounded by the Pacific Ring of Fire – a large number of active volcanoes.

AMAZING!

The Bermuda Triangle

Located in the Atlantic Ocean between Bermuda, Puerto Rico and Florida, the Bermuda Triangle is the site of a number of mysterious incidents involving aeroplanes and boats. People believe that Unidentified Flying Objects (UFOs) are somehow involved and that the mythical continent of Atlantis could be found inside the triangle.

DID YOU KNOW?

Icy cover

The Arctic Ocean is almost completely covered in sea ice during the winter months.

Mariana Trench

The deepest part of the world's oceans and seas is the Mariana Trench, which is located in the western part of the Pacific Ocean, to the east of the Mariana Islands. It is roughly between Japan and Papua New Guinea. It is about 2,550km (1,580 miles) long and reaches a maximum known depth of 10,911km (6,780 miles).

RIVERS AND EROSION

It all starts with a little drip high in the mountains, probably as the warmth of spring melts the mountain snow. The drips form a puddle, which begins to run down the slopes of the mountain in a very small trickle. Several different trickles come together to form a stream and that is how all rivers start…

AMAZING!

Ever-growing rivers

Some rivers remain small, while others (known as tributaries) come together in a fork to form a bigger river. All rivers end in a larger body of water, such as a bigger river, ocean or sea. The place where a river empties its water into a larger body of water is known as the mouth of the river. Sometimes the mouth widens, the speed of the water slows down, and rocks and sand pile up – the mouth develops a fan shape, which is known as a delta.

Erosion

Moving water is very powerful and can wear away soil and rocks. Soil will wash away if there is no vegetation to hold it in place. This movement of rocks and soil is called erosion. Erosion makes rivers muddy after heavy rain and is even responsible for the formation of valleys in mountains.

DID YOU KNOW?

The Grand Canyon

Rivers can create deep grooves in the Earth's surface. These grooves can get deeper and deeper. In time this will create a canyon. The world's most famous canyon is the Grand Canyon in America.

A river life-saver

In 2009 a plane had to make an emergency landing after birds hit the engines. The pilot managed to land the plane in the Hudson River, which runs through New York, saving all lives on board.

AWESOME FACT!

The River Nile

The longest river in the world is the River Nile – it stretches for 6,650km (4,132 miles). The Nile is also one of the few rivers that flows from south to north. The Nile crocodile, one of the world's deadliest animals, lives on the banks of the River Nile.

Monstrous river

The River Amazon in South America is one of the largest and most dangerous rivers in the world. It is not only very long, but also very wide. It is so big that there are no two points that can be crossed by bridge and it is also sometimes called the "River Sea". It is home to a ferocious species of fish called piranha.

Black river

The River Negro, located in South America, is unique because of the unusual colour of its water – the water in this river is black!

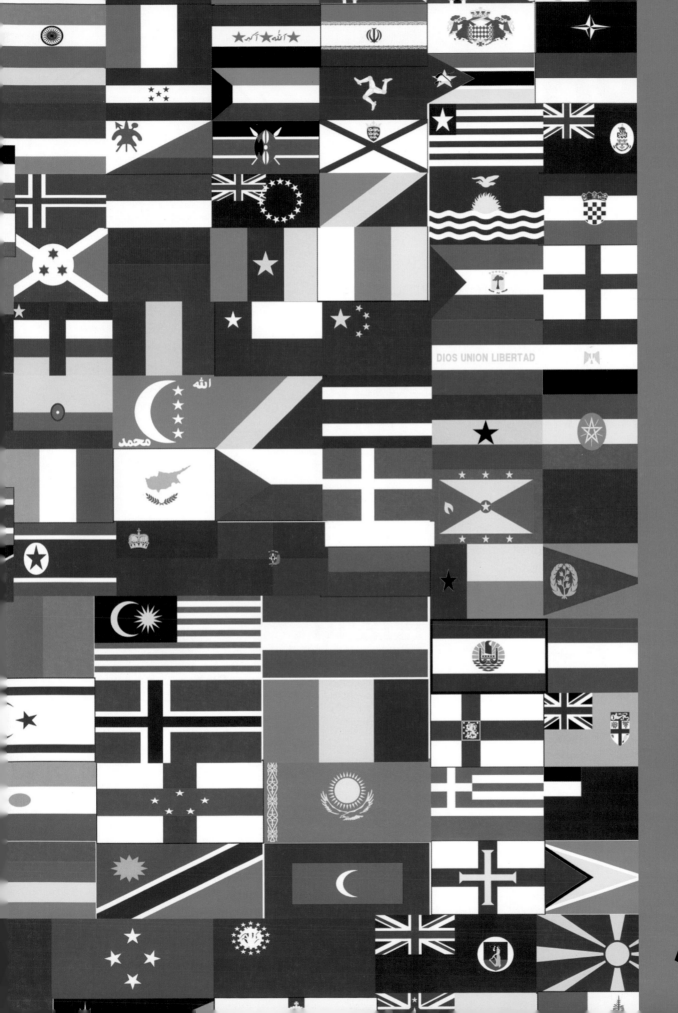

DIOS UNION LIBERTAD

EUROPE

Europe is the sixth largest continent in size and the third largest in terms of population. It is bordered by the Mediterranean Sea to the south, Asia to the east, and the Atlantic Ocean to the west. Europe is very wealthy and also the centre of western democracy.

Old countries

San Marino, France, Bulgaria, Denmark and Portugal are the five oldest countries in the world. They are also all part of the continent of Europe.

The European Union

Lots of European countries have united to form the European Union. This allows the member countries to have a single currency – the euro – and to combine their economic and military power.

A giant among nations

Russia, the largest country in the world, covers 11 time zones and two continents, Asia and Europe.

Island capital

Finland's capital, Helsinki, is the northernmost capital in Europe and stretches across more than 300 islands.

World wars

Two of the biggest wars in modern history took place in Europe: the First World War (1914–1918) and the Second World War (1939–1945).

AMAZING!

Great civilizations

Europe was home to two of the world's greatest civilizations: that of the Ancient Greeks and also the Roman Empire.

Holy place

Europe is the location of the world's smallest country – the Vatican, which is where the Pope lives.

Biggest city

Istanbul, in Turkey, is Europe's biggest city with a population of 13,854,740.

Caspian Sea

The Caspian Sea is the world's largest body of water that is completely surrounded by land. It is even larger than Japan.

Matador

During a bullfight, a popular activity in Spain, a bullfighter called a matador waves a red cape to get a bull to charge at him. Bulls are colour-blind, but the movement of the cape attracts them – and they will charge!

DID YOU KNOW?

Awesome European Facts!

1 SCOTTISH RED

More people with red hair are born in Scotland than anywhere else in the world.

2 CANAL ROADS

Venice, in Italy, has no roads. Instead, the inhabitants use canals to move around. The city is actually made of more than 100 islands connected by a canal system.

3 BICYCLE POPULATION

It's estimated that there are more bicycles than people in Amsterdam, the capital of the Netherlands.

4 SWIM LAW

Every person in Iceland has to learn to swim. It's the law!

5 FOOTBALL CHAMPIONS

The British, Spanish and Italian football leagues are considered to be the best in the world.

6 TOWER PAINT

The Eiffel Tower in Paris, in France, is repainted every seven years. It takes a team of 25 painters using more than 1,500 brushes a year to paint the huge monument.

ASIA

Asia is the world's largest and most populated continent – with over 4 billion people, it is home to 60 per cent of the world's population. Asia is the only continent that borders two other continents: Africa and Europe in the west. The Pacific Ocean sits to its east. Asia has a major influence on the world's economy, with China being one of world's largest economies and exporting products to every country in the world. The oil in the Middle East is a major source of the world's energy.

SCAN ME
Instructions on page 5

Giant lizards

The Komodo dragon (*Varanus komodoensis*) lives on the islands of Indonesia. Komodo dragons are the largest living lizards in the world, reaching a length of 3m (10ft).

DID YOU KNOW?

Billions of people

The world's most populated countries, China and India, are situated on the continent of Asia. Each of them has a population of more than 1 billion people.

Movie ban

Movie theatres are prohibited in Saudi Arabia, as they allow men and women to mingle unsupervised. Many Saudis who live close to the Island of Bahrain drive over there at weekends to watch movies.

Bigger than the Moon

The area of Asia is about 44 million square kilometres (17 million square miles) – that is bigger than the surface of the Moon!

Fancy a game of kokpar?

In Kazakhstan they play a traditional sport called *kokpar* in which two teams on horseback try to move a goat's carcass to a goal in the centre of a field.

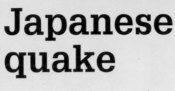

Japanese quake

Japan gets hit by more than 1,000 earthquakes a year and has one of the world's most effective earthquake-warning systems.

Amazing tree hotel

In Vietnam you can stay in a hotel that is carved out of a tree. Some people call it the "Crazy House". All of the rooms have an animal theme, such as the tiger room, eagle room and kangaroo room. The hotel is called Hang Nga and was designed by the female Vietnamese architect Dang Viet Nga.

Religions

Many of the world's religions originated in Asia, including Christianity, Judaism, Hinduism, Islam and Buddhism.

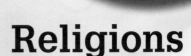

AMAZING!

Rare but dangerous

Some of the world's most endangered and dangerous mammals are found in Asia, including the snow leopard, Asiatic black bear, tigers, orang-utans and the giant panda.

Blue fireworks

The Chinese invented fireworks. Blue-violet fireworks are the hardest to create because the concentrations of chemicals are so unstable and dangerous.

NORTH AMERICA

North America is dominated by its three biggest countries – Mexico, Canada and the United States – but Central America and the Caribbean are also part of this vast continent. It's the world's third largest continent and bordered by the Atlantic Ocean to the east and the Pacific Ocean to the west.

Biggest island

The country of Greenland is the biggest island on the planet, with an area of 2,175,600 square kilometres (840,004 square miles).

Freshwater giant

Lake Superior is the largest freshwater lake in the world. It is located on the border between the United States and Canada.

Scenic route

Before the construction of the Panama Canal, ships had to go around South America to get from the Atlantic Ocean to the Pacific Ocean. Which is a 12,874-km (8,000-mile) round trip! At the height of its construction in 1904, nearly 40,000 people worked on the Panama Canal.

Columbus

Columbus has been given much credit for "discovering" America, but, long before Columbus arrived, many native American tribes and the Aztec civilization already lived there. Furthermore, Columbus never set foot in what is now the United States – he actually landed first in the Bahamas.

Which number are you?

Toronto, in Canada, has the longest street in the world – Yonge Street. It is 1,896km (1,178 miles) long, which is further than the distance from London in England to Madrid in Spain.

Amerigo

North America was named after Amerigo Vespucci, an early explorer of the Americas. He even helped Columbus to prepare for some of his journeys.

SUPER FACT!

Dino killer

Scientists think that dinosaurs died out due to the devastating effects of a meteor which left a 180-km (112-mile) hole in Mexico's Yucatan Peninsula.

DID YOU KNOW?

Amazing American Facts!

1 VOLCANO-FREE ZONE

Honduras is the only country in Central America that doesn't have a volcano.

2 CRYSTAL CAVE

An underground cave in Mexico has the world's largest crystals. The longest one is eight times taller than the average ten-year-old child.

3 OPOSSUM

North America is home to only one species of marsupial – the opossum – which is only active at night.

4 DRIVE-IN

McDonald's started in 1940 in San Bernardino, California, in the United States, as a drive-in restaurant with a car-hop service. They now have 33,000 branches around the world.

5 LOOSE CHANGE?

Americans have a total of about $10 billion in loose change just sitting around their homes.

SOUTH AMERICA

The fourth largest continent in size and the fifth in population is South America. It is bordered, like North America, by the Atlantic and Pacific Oceans. The continent is also dominated by the Andes mountain range and the Amazon River. Most people on the continent speak Spanish or Portuguese because of the Spanish and Portuguese colonisation of the continent during the 1500s.

Galapagos Islands

About 1,000km (620 miles) away from the continental mainland is a very special group of 19 islands called the Galapagos Islands. They are a national park and part of Ecuador. Some unique species of animal, such as the massive Galapagos tortoise (*Geochelone nigra*), live on these islands. The islands helped Charles Darwin to develop his theory of evolution while on his voyage of discovery on board HMS *Beagle*.

INTERESTING

Finger monkeys

The rainforests of South America are home to the world's smallest monkey, the pygmy marmoset (*Cebuella pygmaea*). It is only 13cm (5in) tall. These monkeys are also known as "finger monkeys".

Butterfly forest

The South American rainforests are home to a quarter of all butterfly species on Earth. The biggest butterfly in South America is the owl butterfly. Reaching 14cm (5½ in) across, it is about the same size as the hand of a large man.

Fun-filled carnival!

The world's biggest and best-known party takes place every year in Brazil. The Brazilian Carnival marks the beginning of Lent, the 40-day period before Easter. It lasts five days and the big cities have massive, multi-coloured parades going through the streets.

Floating families

In Lake Titicaca people live on artificial islands made out of woven reeds. Ten families can easily live on the larger islands. These were originally built as a means of defence so that people could easily move on to them in case of threat.

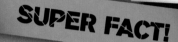

SUPER FACT!

Castaway

Robinson Crusoe, a book by Daniel Defoe published in 1719, tells the story of a castaway stranded on a tropical island. The tale was inspired by the life of a real man who was shipwrecked on an island off the coast of Chile.

Bottle dance

A kind of dance in Paraguay is called the *Gallopa* which involves women balancing bottles on their heads as they dance.

Ant snack

One of Colombia's most popular snacks is called *Hormiga Culona* or roasted ants.

Working animals

Llamas and vicunas are related to camels, but don't have a hump. The wool of the vicuna is used to make clothes because it is very soft. Llamas are used as pack animals, but if too much weight is added to their load they will refuse to move!

AFRICA

Africa is the second largest continent in terms of both area and population. It borders the Mediterranean Sea to the north, the Atlantic Ocean to the west, Asia to the north-east, and the Indian Ocean to the south-east. Africa has a population of 1.1 billion people, belonging to more than 3,000 ethnic groups and speaking more than 2,000 languages. Sudan is Africa's largest country and the smallest is the Seychelles.

AMAZING!

Giraffe stacking

Mount Kilimanjaro is Africa's tallest mountain, reaching a height of 5,895m (19,340ft). That's the equivalent of roughly 1,018 adult giraffes stacked on top of each other!

Lake Victoria

Lake Victoria is the largest lake in Africa and the second largest freshwater lake in the whole world, covering an area of 69,490 square kilometres (26,830 square miles). That's almost as big as Scotland!

A place of evolution

Africa is widely considered to be the continent where human beings first evolved, around 200,000 years ago.

Record-holders!

The wildlife in Africa is record-breaking. The African elephant is the world's largest land animal, the giraffe is the world's tallest animal, the cheetah is the world's fastest land animal, and the gorilla is the world's largest primate.

Nobel winners

Ten African leaders have won the Nobel Peace Prize. Nelson Mandela and Frederik de Klerk were the last to win jointly in 1993 for all their peace work in South Africa.

DID YOU KNOW?

A land with no rivers

Libya, a country in North Africa, is one of the few countries in the world that has no natural rivers.

INTERESTING!

Madagascar

Three-quarters of the animals on Madagascar, the world's fourth largest island, are found nowhere else on Earth. Lemurs are one of the most well known of these.

Pyramids

Although Egypt is world famous for its mightly pyramids, Sudan has far more. They are, however, much smaller.

SUPER FACT!

It's a real gold mine!

Most of the gold and diamonds in the world come from African mines. More than half the gold ever mined on Earth has come from mines near the city of Johannesburg, in South Africa.

AUSTRALASIA

Australasia is also known as Oceania or simply Australia, but this continent includes more countries than just Australia. Australasia is the smallest continent based on size and the second smallest continent in terms of population. It is made up of Australia and numerous other islands, all of which are surrounded by the Indian and Pacific Oceans. Most of Australasia's land is desert and volcano.

INTERESTING!

Down under

Australia and New Zealand are often called the "Land Down Under" because of their location in the Southern Hemisphere. Australasia is the only continent that is positioned completely south of the Equator.

New arrivals

Nearly a quarter of the people who live in Australia were born in another country. The first English settlers arrived in 1788, but the Aboriginal people, the native inhabitants of Australia, have lived on the continent for 60,000 years.

Unique wildlife

Australasia has some unique animals for a small continent. Animals such as koalas (*Phascolarctos cinereus*) and kangaroos are only found there. The only egg-laying mammal lives there too – the much-loved platypus (*Ornithorhynchus anatinus*).

DID YOU KNOW?

Taupo

The largest volcanic eruption ever recorded in history took place in Taupo, in New Zealand, about 26,500 years ago. The eruption reached 50km (30 miles) into the sky.

DID YOU KNOW?

Prison colony

Australia was first colonised in the late 18th century by Europeans who used it as a penal or prison colony.

Multi-lingual

People in Papua New Guinea speak more than 700 languages, the highest number of any country in the world.

AWESOME FACT

Fire protection

The tough bark of the eucalyptus tree protects it from dangerous fires, which can happen naturally in Australia and frequently occur in dry areas.

DID YOU KNOW?

Awesome Facts about Australasia

1 ANIMAL POPULATION

Australia has more sheep and kangaroos living on the island than people.

2 EMU

Australia's fastest bird, the emu, can't fly, but can run as fast as 64 km/h (40 mph). When attacked by birds of prey, emus run in a zigzag pattern.

3 UNIQUE PLANTS

About 90 per cent of the plants that grow in New Zealand are found nowhere else in the world.

4 SECOND WORLD WAR TREASURES

In Papua New Guinea, sunken ships from the Second World War are a popular attraction for scuba divers.

ANTARCTICA AND THE ARCTIC

The Arctic is not strictly a continent, but a region, made up of parts of Russia, Greenland, Canada, the United States, Norway, Iceland, Sweden and Finland. It's also known as the North Pole and has a native population, the Inuit, who live in the North American part.

Antarctica is the fifth largest continent in size, but the smallest in terms of population – this is officially zero! Antarctica, which is surrounded by the Southern Ocean, is also known as the South Pole and is the coldest, driest continent on Earth. The Arctic is not a continent, but a region, made up of parts of Russia, Greenland, Canada, the United States, Norway, Iceland, Sweden and Finland. Also known as the North Pole, it has a native population called the Inuit.

Captain Scott

Captain Robert Falcon Scott first explored Antarctica on board *The Discovery* during the expedition of 1901–1904. Another great British Antarctic explorer, Ernest Shackleton, was chosen to join him. Scott later reached the South Pole on 17 January 1912, a month after Norwegian Roald Amundsen. Scott and his team perished on their return journey.

Untouched discovery

Antarctica was first discovered in the 1820s, but it took another 75 years before anyone actually set foot on it.

Norwegian Roald Amundsen was the first person to reach both the North and South Poles. He arrived at the South Pole on 14 December 1911 and reached the North Pole in 1926.

SCAN ME
Instructions on page 5

Winter birds

Emperor penguins (*Aptenodytes forsteri*) are the only warm-blooded animals that remain on Antarctica for the winter. They are also the only bird that breeds in winter. Male emperor penguins balance an egg on their feet for about two months to keep it warm.

AWESOME FACT!

Icebergs

When you look at an iceberg, you can only see about 10 per cent of it sitting above the water's surface because most of an iceberg is hidden under water. The largest iceberg measured in the Antarctic was 335km (208 miles) long by 97km (60 miles) wide, which is slightly larger than Belgium.

Slow grower

Lichens, a type of plant, are adapted to the cold climate of Antarctica. They grow very slowly at a rate of about 1cm (½in) every 1,000 years.

Freezing mammals

Antarctica has a lot of sea mammals, seals and whales, but there are no land mammals.

Neanderthal fossil

In 2011, Neanderthal remains found near the Arctic Circle were dated at over 28,500 years old. This is more than 8,000 years after Neanderthals are thought to have disappeared.

Long summer's day

During the summer the Sun is always up in the Arctic. The Sun rises in March and sets in September. That's a really long summer's day!

Amazing Facts about Antarctica and the Arctic

1 FRESH ICE

More than 99 per cent of Antarctica is covered with ice – the ice cap holds 70 per cent of the world's fresh water.

2 FLOODS

If all the ice in Antarctica melted, the oceans would rise by 60m (197ft).

3 TIMELESS

Antarctica doesn't have any time zones. Every researcher and visitor on the continent has to use his or her own home time.

4 ICE MONEY

Although there are no people living in Antarctica, there are still some ATM machines!

5 NATURAL ANTI-FREEZE

Antarctic cod (*Dissostichus mawsoni*), a type of fish, can survive in icy waters because it produces a natural anti-freeze in its blood.

THE WORLD'S COUNTRIES

Some countries are not much bigger than a city, while others are as big as a whole continent with a lot of states or provinces. Some countries may be ruled by a different country which lies on the other side of the world. There are about 195 countries in the world, but it is difficult to give a precise figure. New countries keep appearing, perhaps as a result of provinces or cultural groups breaking away from a country. Diplomatic negotiations between countries decide whether those new countries are recognised.

DID YOU KNOW?

The Age of Discovery

Between the 15th and 17th centuries many countries in Europe sent out explorers to discover new lands, find trade routes, look for treasure, and gain territory for their country. The world was mapped out and many civilizations came into contact with each other during this golden Age of Exploration, which is also known as the Age of Discovery.

Growth of the colonies

During the Age of Exploration many explorers claimed the land they found in the name of their country. Most of the Americas, Africa and Australia were taken over as colonies by European countries like Spain, Portugal and Great Britain.

What is an empire?

An empire is made up of different colonies around the world owned by a parent country. The emperor or king rules over these different colonies or nations, which were originally claimed by the country's explorers. With countries ruling over a growing number of colonies, big empires were eventually created. At its height in the early 1900s, for example, the British Empire was one of the world's largest empires, which remained intact until after the Second World War.

Famous British explorers

Sir Walter Raleigh, a British explorer who led many expeditions to America, is thought to have introduced potatoes and tobacco to Britain.

Sir Francis Drake was the first Englishman to sail around the world. He was a brilliant sailor and helped England become a major sea power in the 16th century.

The power of alliances

Countries all over the world sometimes come together for common causes. These unions are called alliances, which pursue shared goals. These include the United Nations (UN), which was set up just after the Second World War to promote world peace. The African Union tries to reduce conflict and poverty across the African continent, while the World Bank was founded in 1944 to help rebuild post-war Europe and to give financial assistance to the poorest nations.

The Commonwealth

A growing number of British colonies gained independence in the second half of the 20th century. This was when the British Commonwealth was developed. This alliance is not a political one, but its 54 independent members share values and strong trade links. They also work to promote democracy, human rights and world peace.

INTERESTING

The European Union

After the Second World War, European countries decided to work together to resolve their problems in a European Union (EU). About 50 years later, the EU has 27 member states and more countries are trying to join. Within the Union goods, services and people can move freely and most of the countries even use the same currency – the Euro.

WHAT MAKES COUNTRIES UNIQUE?

The world has big countries and small countries, monarchies and republics, but what really makes a country unique is its history. Every country has its own story to tell which is mostly the result of achieving full, or a degree of, independence, a flag, a currency, a national costume and a unique language.

DID YOU KNOW?

Dannebrog

Denmark has the world's oldest flag, the Dannebrog. This started out as a banner for Danish crusaders in the beginning of the 13th century.

Beautiful Belize

The flag of Belize contains twelve colours, three more than any other national flag. It is also the only country to have humans on the flag.

Plain green

There is just one flag in the world that uses only one colour and has no other design features. This belongs to the country of Libya. The flag, which was adopted in 1977, is completely green with no other defining characteristics.

How much?

Once in Zimbabwe, you were able to pay for things with a 100 trillion Zimbabwe dollar note. The actual value of the note was only about £3.25. In those times you had to pay 700 million Zimbabwe dollars for a loaf of bread.

The world's largest coin

The largest coin currently in circulation is the Australian 50 cent piece. It measures 35mm (1½ in) across.

Old money

Pounds sterling is the world's oldest currency that is still in use. However, the current pound is dramatically different from the pound as it was defined in 1526.

A lot of talk

The most widely spoken language on the planet is Mandarin, a Chinese language. Speaking Mandarin is really difficult, though, as every word can be pronounced in four different ways. Over one billion people speak the language. To say hello in Mandarin, you say: "Ni hao" (which is pronounced Nee HaOW).

Ancient language

Recent archaeological evidence has shown that Tamil could have been the language used by the Indus people, a Bronze Age civilization (3,300–1,300 BC) living in the north-western region of India. The language is still in use in the area today, which makes Tamil the oldest living language in the world.

Speechless?

The English language has about 600,000 words registered in the *Oxford English Dictionary*, but new words are being added all the time. This makes English one of the world's most word-heavy languages.

CITIES AROUND THE WORLD

Until recently most people in the world lived in rural areas. Now many people live in cities in the hope of finding new opportunities. But this has led to overcrowding and the growth of slums at the edges of some big cities in developing countries. Poor hygiene, unsafe drinking water, and poor-quality housing make these slums dangerous places to live and far removed from the dreams people had when they first moved to the city. However, most western cities thrive and become desirable economic centres.

SUPER FACTS ABOUT LONDON

Roman giant

Built on the banks of the River Thames by the Romans, who called it Londinium, London is now one of Europe's biggest cities. London is home to about 12 per cent of Britain's population.

The Shard

London's highest building is The Shard. At a height of 310m (1,017ft), it is also Europe's tallest building.

First tube

London was the first city to have an underground railway, which is called the London Underground.

SUPER FACTS ABOUT PARIS

Perfect destination

Paris, the capital of France, is one of the world's leading cultural cities, known for its artistic inhabitants. Paris is also one of the most visited cities in the world, with touristic attractions including the Eiffel tower, Notre Dame Cathedral and the Champ-Elysées.

Le beau soleil!

No building in Paris is allowed by law to be higher than six storeys because the French believe that everyone should be able to enjoy the sun (soleil).

Pampered pooches

There are more dogs in Paris than children. Around 300,000 dogs live in Paris. There are even special dog shops, equipped with clothes, socks, shoes, diamond collars and even wardrobes for dogs.

SUPER FACTS ABOUT SYDNEY

Cultural melting-pot

Sydney is home to about 20 per cent of the Australian population with around 4.6 million people living in Australia's most iconic city. It is a melting-pot of cultures, with the largest cultural groups being British, Chinese, New Zealanders, Vietnamese, Lebanese, Filipinos and Italians.

Opera House

Sydney's most famous icon is the Sydney Opera House, which was completed in 1973. Ten thousand construction workers took 14 years to build it.

SUPER FACTS ABOUT NEW YORK

"The Big Apple"

New York is America's most populated city. Also known as "The Big Apple or "the city that never sleeps", millions of people visit New York for the culture, world-class cuisine and exciting nightlife.

The Subway

New York's Underground (or subway) is the largest mass-transit system in the world with 468 stations, 1,355km (842 miles) of track, and an average of 4.9 million people using it each weekday. The New York Subway runs for 24 hours a day.

FAMOUS BUILDINGS

Man has created some pretty impressive buildings over the years, including those with historical value, as well as lots of buildings in the ongoing competition to build the world's tallest building.

The Statue of Liberty

It took nine years, with men working 10 hours a day, seven days a week, to construct the Statue of Liberty. Although it is now a symbol of American culture, it was originally a gift from France to America. The Statue has size 879 sandals, each measuring 7.6m (25ft).

The Taj Mahal

The Taj Mahal is a famous mausoleum in Agra, India. A mausoleum is a building that contains burial chambers for the deceased. The Taj Mahal was originally built as resting place for the third wife of the Mughal Emperor Shah Jahan and took 20 years to build. It is made completely of white marble and considered to be one of the Seven Wonders of the World.

DID YOU KNOW?

The Great Wall of China

Once built to protect China's northern boundaries, at a length of 3,460km (2,145 miles), the Great Wall is the longest man-made structure in the world. Sadly, the wall does not go on forever and Mongol invaders, led by Genghis Khan, had no problem going round the wall and invading most of northern China between 1211 and 1223.

The Leaning Tower of Pisa

Inspired by the minarets on mosques, the Italians built this bell tower for the Cathedral of Pisa. It held a bell that would ring to tell people to come to church. However, the builders weren't very experienced and built the tower on soft ground. As soon as the tower was finished, it began to tilt slowly to one side.

The Shard

Europe's tallest building, reaching 310m (1,017ft), is in London and called The Shard. It has 44 lifts, including double-decker lifts, and 306 flights of stairs.

Burj Khalifa

Burj Khalifa is the world's tallest building, reaching a colossal height of 828.9m (2,719ft). Located in downtown Dubai, it opened in 2010 after taking six years to build. It has 160 floors.

The Eiffel Tower

The Eiffel Tower in Paris was originally built as the entrance arch to the World Exhibition of 1889. Not everyone liked the tower when it was first built, however, because of its bold design. But over 250 million people have visited the Eiffel Tower since it opened. It is 320m (1,050ft) tall.

The Plant Kingdom

4

THE WORLD OF TREES

Trees are the largest types of plant in the plant kingdom. Some are thousands of years old, while others are taller than the Statue of Liberty in New York. All trees can be divided in two basic groups: broad-leaved trees, which are mostly found in temperate climate zones, and needle-leaved trees that are found in colder or drier climate zones. Palm trees make up a third, much smaller, group.

AMAZING!

Drive-through redwoods

The redwood trees of Northern California, in the United States, are the biggest trees in the world. Many of them were already there when Christopher Columbus first arrived in America. The trees are s huge along the highway running through the Humboldt Redwood State Park that people have carved tunnels in those which are larg enough for a car to drive through. This is easier than cutting them down! The highway is known as "The Avenue of Giants".

SUPER FACT!

World's tallest tree

In 2006 two naturalists, Chris Atkins and Michael Taylor, found a coast redwood tree (*Sequoia sempervirens*) that reached a height of 115.55m (379ft 1in), making it the world's tallest tree. They called the tree *Hyperion*. Since then it has grown a little more and now measures an astounding 115.61m (379ft 3in). The exact location of this mighty tree is being kept a secret to protect it from tourists who may accidentally damage the tree's surroundings and harm its growth.

AMAZING!

Rings of age

Each year a tree will produce another layer of wood around its trunk. When the tree is cut down, you can count the rings in the trunk and then work out the age of the tree.

Needle-leaf trees

The needles of some evergreen trees, such as pines, firs and yews, are actually mini leaves. The thick skin, waterproof wax coating and shape of the needles all help to reduce the rate of water evaporation from the leaves. This enables evergreen trees such as these to save water, which is vital they are to survive the tough conditions in the habitats in which they grow.

Leafy shapes

Leaves come in a variety of shapes. The leaves also have differently shaped edges and are arranged in different ways on the stems of plants. The veins in the leaves are arranged in different ways, too.

Deciduous trees

Most broad-leaved trees are deciduous, which means they shed their leaves seasonally. Deciduous trees do not need their leaves for photosynthesis in the winter and go into a period of dormancy until the following spring.

Ancient trees

The root system of "Old Tjikko", a type of Norway spruce (*Picea abies*) discovered in the Fulu Mountains in Sweden, is believed to have been growing for around 9,550 years. It would have taken root just after the last Ice Age. The roots produce new trees after each one dies.

The oldest standing tree is a bristlecone pine (*Pinus longaeva*) called *Methuselah*, which has been growing in California's White Mountains for about 4,600 years.

Amazing Tree Facts

1 AUTUMN GLORY

In the autumn, New England, in the United States, is a prime tourist destination, as the woods and forests blaze with dazzling autumn colours.

2 SPRING BLOSSOM

Many cities in Japan, including Tokyo, Kyoto and Osaka, are famous for their breathtaking displays of tree blossom in spring. The traditional Japanese custom of flower viewing is called *hanami*.

3 SALTY WATER

Mangroves are the only trees that can grow in salt water. They have developed special roots to help them absorb oxygen from water.

4 MOST DROUGHT-RESISTANT TREE

The baobab tree (*Adansonia digitata*) from Africa can store up to 136,000 litres (29,900 gallons) of water in its trunk.

THE BEAUTY OF FLOWERS

Many plants produce beautiful flowers in a range of colours. Some flowers also have a gorgeous fragrance. Colour and fragrance are important to plants that depend on attracting insects such as bees and butterflies to pollinate their flowers. Flowerless plants rely on wind for reproduction, which is a less efficient.

The flower of love

The rose is the international flower of love, but did you know that the colours of roses can be used to send messages? **Red** means love, **yellow** means happiness, **white** denotes purity, **pink** represents appreciation, **peach** is for optimism, and **purple** stands for love at first sight.

Flower anatomy

A flower has three main parts: the petals, carpel and stamen. The carpel is the female part of the flower, which is made up the ovary, style and stigma. The stamen is the male part of the flower and is made up of the anther and filament.

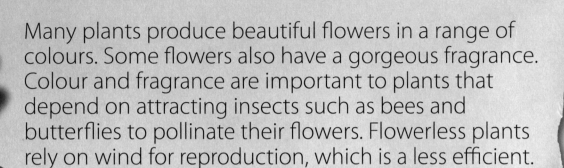

Anther

The anther is loaded with pollen grains, which are taken away by the wind or by feeding insects.

Filament

A filament supports each anther.

Sepals

Sepals make up the gre ring around the peta Sepals protect the flov when it is in bud.

Stigma

The stigma is sticky and traps the pollen carried to the flower by visiting insects.

Style

The ovary extends into a style. This carries the stigma.

Petals

Brightly coloured petals encourage insects to visit flowers. The petals drop as soon as the flower is fertilized.

Golden tulip

In 17th-century Holland, tulip bulbs were highly prized and more valuable than gold. The flower symbolized immortality, life and love.

Language of flowers

Flowers are popular gifts, but many flowers can also be used to send messages. The sending of flowers with symbolic names was popular with the Victorians.

❖ **Gardenias** mean "I'm secretly in love with you".

❖ **Daisies** symbolise love, innocence, purity and loyalty.

❖ **Tulips** represent charity.

❖ **Hydrangeas** mean heartlessness or thank you for understanding.

❖ **Sunflowers** mean best wishes and loyalty.

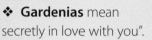
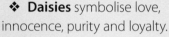
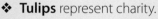

Giant flowers

The Titan arum (*Amorphophallus titanum*) has huge flowers that can reach 3m (10ft) high and 90cm (3ft) wide. The flowers smell of decaying flesh and are therefore known as corpse flowers.

Awesome Flower Facts

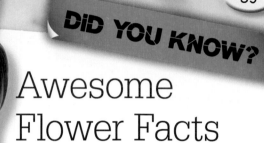

1 FLOWER OF DEATH

Agave plants can live for many years without producing any flowers. Sadly, an agave will die after producing one single flower.

2 MOON FLOWERS

Night-blooming flowers such as some species of *Ipomoea* bloom at night and close during the day.

3 HAVE WE RUN OUT OF ONIONS?

In some recipes, you can replace onions with tulips. Don't try this at home!

4 BLIND SPOT

Bright reds and pinks are more attractive to birds than insects because not all insects can see red.

FRUIT

Plants produce fruit to hold their seeds. Animals eat the fruit and carry the seeds away in their stomach. The seeds have tough skins and so are not digested by the animal. Instead, the seeds pass out with the animal's droppings, far from the parent plant. The seeds then germinate and grow into new plants.

Veggie fruit

Lots of people think that tomatoes are a type of vegetable. However, tomatoes are actually a fruit. The tomato is, in fact, one of the most popular types of fruit in the world. Peppers, aubergines and pumpkins are also fruits that are eaten as vegetables

AMAZING!

DID YOU KNOW?

Imposter berry

Despite its name, a strawberry is not really a berry. The name comes from the children that first sold the fruit in the 19th century. The children picked the strawberries, strung them on grass straws, and then sold them as "straws of berries". The strawberry is the only fruit that carries its seeds on the outside.

A rainbow of health

Eating more fruit can significantly reduce the risk of chronic diseases such as obesity, heart disease and some cancers. Every fruit colour has its own remedy:

Blue/purple fruit helps your memory, **green** fruit make your bones and teeth stronger, **yellow** fruit stops you getting sick, orange fruit keeps your eyes healthy, and **red** fruit keeps your heart strong.

Durian fruit

Many fruits have a fragrance that attracts foraging animals. The durian fruit from South-East Asia has a particularly strong smell. It is so strong that you either love it or hate it! It is also the biggest fruit in the world.

Avocadoes

Avocado leaves are harmful to animals and the fruits may be poisonous to some birds. A study has shown that, although the avocado is the most nutritious of all fruits, it also has the highest fat content.

Citrus trees

Citrus trees grow in warm Mediterranean climates and bear colourful, juicy fruits. The fruits may be sweet or tart. Citrus fruits have a very thick, waxy skin in yellow, orange or green. Examples include limes, lemons, oranges and grapefruits. The fruits are rich in vitamin C.

Apple choice

All over the world people grow over 7,000 different varieties of apple. Golden Delicious and Gala apples are the most popular.

Chocolate fruit

The cacao tree (*Theobroma cacao*) grows in the rainforests of the Amazon and Orinoco and produces a fruit called a pod. Each pod contains 20 to 60 seeds – these are cocoa beans, which are used to make chocolate.

VEGETABLES AND FOOD PLANTS

Many plants form a very important part of our daily diet. Not only do vegetables such as potatoes and crops like cereals come from plants, but so do drinks like tea and coffee. Although you can sometimes eat all of a plant, it's more common to eat just one delicious part. For example, we eat flowers like broccoli and cauliflower, stems such as asparagus and rhubarb, seeds like corn, peas and nuts, the leaves of cabbages and lettuce, and, finally, the roots of carrots, radishes and beetroot.

AWESOME FACT!

All change

Carrots were originally purple, red, yellow or white. Orange carrots were first grown in the 16th century when the Dutch crossbred red and yellow carrots to create an orange carrot in honour of their Royal Family, which is known as the House of Orange.

Dangerous food!

Who said vegetables are good for your health? In the United Kingdom, in 2005, 14,149 people had to go to hospital with an injury caused by a vegetable.

INTERESTING!

Potatoes

Potatoes originated from South America where they grow in the Andes Mountains. Nowadays, however, China is the world's main producer of potatoes. Popular potato varieties are King Edward and Maris Piper.

Exercise vegetable

Celery is the perfect snack if you are watching your weight. This is because it takes more calories to eat a stick of celery than it contains – so, you literally slim while you eat!

Other Food Plants

Wheat

Wheat is one of the oldest known crops. It was first cultivated over 6,000 years ago in Mesopotamia (which is present-day Iraq). Many crop plants originate from the Middle East, including peas, lentils, onions, figs, apples and pears.

Coffee

Coffee is produced from the berries of a large shrub. The most commonly used coffee is *Coffea arabica*. The berries, known as coffee beans, are dried and the beans are roasted once the flesh and seeds have been removed.

Tea

Around 2,737 BC a Chinese emperor boiled some water under a tree. One of the tree's leaves fell into the pot and the emperor loved the taste. So, the drink tea was discovered by accident. All tea comes from a plant called *Camellia sinensis*, a shrub native to China. Different teas, such as Lapsang Souchong and Earl Grey, are produced by processing the harvested leaves differently.

Corn

Farmers grow corn on every continent except for Antarctica. Corn is America's main field crop and is also used in most dried pet food. The corn-cob is part of the corn plant's flower.

Rice

Rice is grown in flooded paddy fields which cover large areas of the Tropics. Asia produces 90 per cent of the world's rice.

Amazing Vegetable Facts

1 WORLD'S BIGGEST MARROW

In 2008 Ken Dade grew the world's largest marrow in Norfolk, in the United Kingdom. It weighed 65kg (143lb) and required two men to carry it.

2 WORLD'S HOTTEST CHILLI PEPPERS

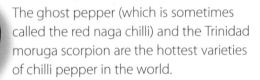

The ghost pepper (which is sometimes called the red naga chilli) and the Trinidad moruga scorpion are the hottest varieties of chilli pepper in the world.

3 THE GREEN STATE

California produces nearly all the broccoli sold in the United States.

4 NIGHT VISION

Carrots really do help you to see in the dark because they contain beta-carotene. This substance is rich in vitamin A, which is essential for healthy vision.

FUNGI

People used to think that fungi were plants, but we now know that they differ from plants in important ways. The most common fungi are the mushrooms we eat on pizza or in a mushroom sauce. Other members of the fungi family are moulds, truffles and yeast.

Parasites

Mushrooms don't have any chlorophyll and are therefore unable to make their own food. So, they feed on a host, which can be either a plant or an animal. Many species of fungi will obtain food from dead organisms.

Fungi friend or foe?

Some fungi live on trees. We call a fungus **parasitic** when it damages the tree it is growing on. Fungi that help the tree grow are called **symbiotic**.

Single-cell fungus

Yeast is a single-celled fungus that is used to make bread rise and for creating the alcohol in beer, wine and cider through the process of fermentation.

Ceps

Multi-functional mushrooms

The use of mushrooms in food and medicines is well known. However, fungi are also used in the production of pesticides and oils.

AMAZING!

Spore dispersal

Mushrooms use spores to multiply. Some mushrooms use fragrance to attract animals to spread the spores. Stinkhorn mushrooms smell of rotting meat, which attracts flies that then carry the spores away.

Helpful fungi

Fungi have a very negative image. However, there are lots of good fungi, which are used in various medications and to help farmers kill pests.

Largest fungus

The largest living fungus was discovered in an ancient American forest. The honey mushroom fungus *Armillaria ostoyae* stretched 5.6km (3½ miles) across, which is an area as large as 1,665 football fields. It is estimated to be about 2,400 years old.

DID YOU KNOW?

Awesome Fungi Facts

AMAZING!

Expensive fungus

Truffles are fungi that grow on the roots of trees and plants. In the past people used pigs to hunt for truffles, but nowadays dogs are used more often. Truffles are considered a delicacy and are very expensive. In 2010 Italian Stanley Ho paid about £213,000 (US$ 330,000) for a gigantic Italian white alba truffle (*Tuber magnatum*) at a truffle auction in Hong Kong. It weighed 1.36kg (3lb) and is the most expensive truffle ever sold.

Fly agaric

1 KILLER MOULD

When you inhale black mould, it will start growing in your lungs. Eventually, it will kill you.

2 SLEEPING BEAUTIES

If provided with the right conditions, some mushrooms can stay dormant for centuries.

3 MOULDY CHEESE

The blue veins in Stilton cheese and other blue cheeses, as well as the white rind on Brie and Camembert, are actually fungi. Disgusting when you think about it, but it makes them taste really good!

HOW PLANTS MAKE FOOD

Like all living organisms, plants need food for energy – in order to grow, to replace worn-out cells, to get rid of waste products, and to reproduce themselves. Plants are the only living organisms in the world that are able to make their own food, a process that is called photosynthesis.

Photosynthesis – a difficult word

Photosynthesis sounds very difficult, but it is easier if you break it down into two parts. *Photo* is the Greek word for "light" and *synthesis* is Greek for "putting together". So, photosynthesis means plants putting things together using light.

DID YOU KNOW?

The process of photosynthesis

A plant needs three things for photosynthesis to take place: carbon dioxide, water and light. Carbon dioxide is a gas in the air and makes up most of the air we breathe out. It is also one of the gases that scientists believe is causing global warming. Plants breathe in carbon dioxide through tiny mouths (called stomates) in their leaves, suck up water with their roots, and use light from the sun.

Scientists have turned the process of photosynthesis into a simple equation:

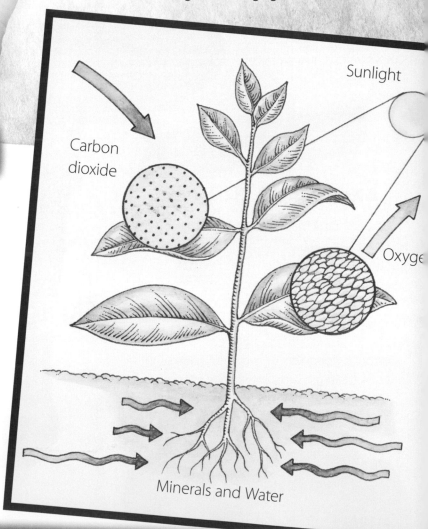

Sunlight

Carbon dioxide

Oxyge

Minerals and Water

Energy from Sunlight

Carbon dioxide + Water ------------------- = Glucose + Oxygen

Chloroplasts

The green leaves of plants are made up of tiny cells and in those cells are little things called chloroplasts. Not only does the chlorophyll in the chloroplasts give plants their green colour, but the chloroplasts are also the place where carbon dioxide, water and light come together to photosynthesise. The chloroplasts change the carbon dioxide, water and sunlight into sugar and oxygen. Plants use the sugar for food and breathe out the oxygen into the atmosphere. That is why plants are so important for Planet Earth.

In partnership with plants

Humans and other animals do exactly the opposite to plants, using oxygen and breathing out carbon dioxide. In other words, we give plants carbon dioxide, while they give us oxygen. Without plants we wouldn't be able to live on Earth, but, without us, there would still be enough carbon dioxide in the atmosphere for plants to exist.

SCAN ME
Instructions on page 5

Carnivorous plants

Some plants live in soils that don't give the plants all of the nutrients they need. So, these plants have developed ways of eating small creatures such as insects. We call these plants carnivorous or insectivorous plants. Examples include the Venus flytrap (*Dionaea muscipula*), pitcher plants, and bladderworts (*Utricularia*), which trap insects and then close tighter and tighter around them. Acids are then produced on the inner surface of the plant to kill and dissolve the unlucky insect.

AMAZING!

A perfect balance

Carbon dioxide is a greenhouse gas, which means that it holds the heat of the Sun close to the Earth. It makes our planet warm and the Earth would be cold like the Moon without it. If there were too much carbon dioxide in the atmosphere, the Earth would become much warmer, like the planet Venus. Plants work hard to keep a perfect balance by turning excess carbon dioxide into oxygen.

USEFUL MATERIALS FROM PLANTS

Plants not only provide us with oxygen and food, but also with lots of other useful things such as woods, oils and cotton. Useful commodities like this are called raw materials. We only use certain parts of some plants, such as the trunk or fruit, but we use other plants completely.

AMAZING!

Musical trees

The wood of maple and spruce trees is used to make the body of violins and contributes to the beautiful sound of these string instruments.

Jojoba

Jojoba is a shrub native to the Sonoran and Mojave deserts of California, Arizona and Mexico. The fruits produce a high-grade oily wax, which is used as a lubricant in printing inks, as well as in lotions and shampoo.

Palm baskets

Raffia is a natural fibre that is made from the young leaves of *Raphia* palms, a genus of palms that largely grows in tropical Africa. Raffia is used to make string and in handcrafts such as basketry.

World's lightest timber

The lightest timber in the world comes from the balsa tree (*Ochroma lagopus*). This wood is so light that it can float very well in water. Balsa trees grow in tropical America. The wood is used to make models, such as aeroplanes, and also for building rafts, for making lifebelts and as a form of insulation.

Bamboo – a versatile material

One of the world's most useful plant products is bamboo. Bamboo is used for building scaffolding and houses, as well as for making furniture and paper. Even pipes and walking sticks can be made from bamboo. When split, it can also be used to make mats, hats, blinds and umbrellas. Bamboo is fast-growing, very strong and easy to grow. Young bamboo shoots are also very tasty – they make up the staple diet of the giant panda!

Soft cotton socks

Cotton is a soft fibre that grows naturally around the seeds of the cotton plant (*Gossypium*), forming bolls. These bolls are picked, ginned to remove the seeds, spun or twisted into thread, and then woven to make cloth. Cotton is also known as "vegetable wool".

Biofuels

As our oil reserves dwindle every day, other sources of fuel need to be found. Oilseed rape (*Brassica napus*), soya bean (*Glycine max*) and the petroleum nut tree (*Pittosporum resiniferum*) in South-East Asia can all be used as plant fuels or biofuels. *Copaifera* trees in the Amazon rainforest hold an oil similar to diesel that can be used to run engines. These biofuels are expected to become increasingly important.

Rubber

Rubber is a material that can be manipulated and stretched, and then return to its original shape. Rubber comes from the rubber tree (*Hevea brasiliensis*). After slivers of the bark are removed, latex flows out of the tree and is collected in receptacles attached to the tree. The latex is treated so that it can be used as rubber in products such as mats, pencil erasers, inflatable objects like dinghies, and rubber types. Beside natural rubber, a synthetic rubber has been developed as well.

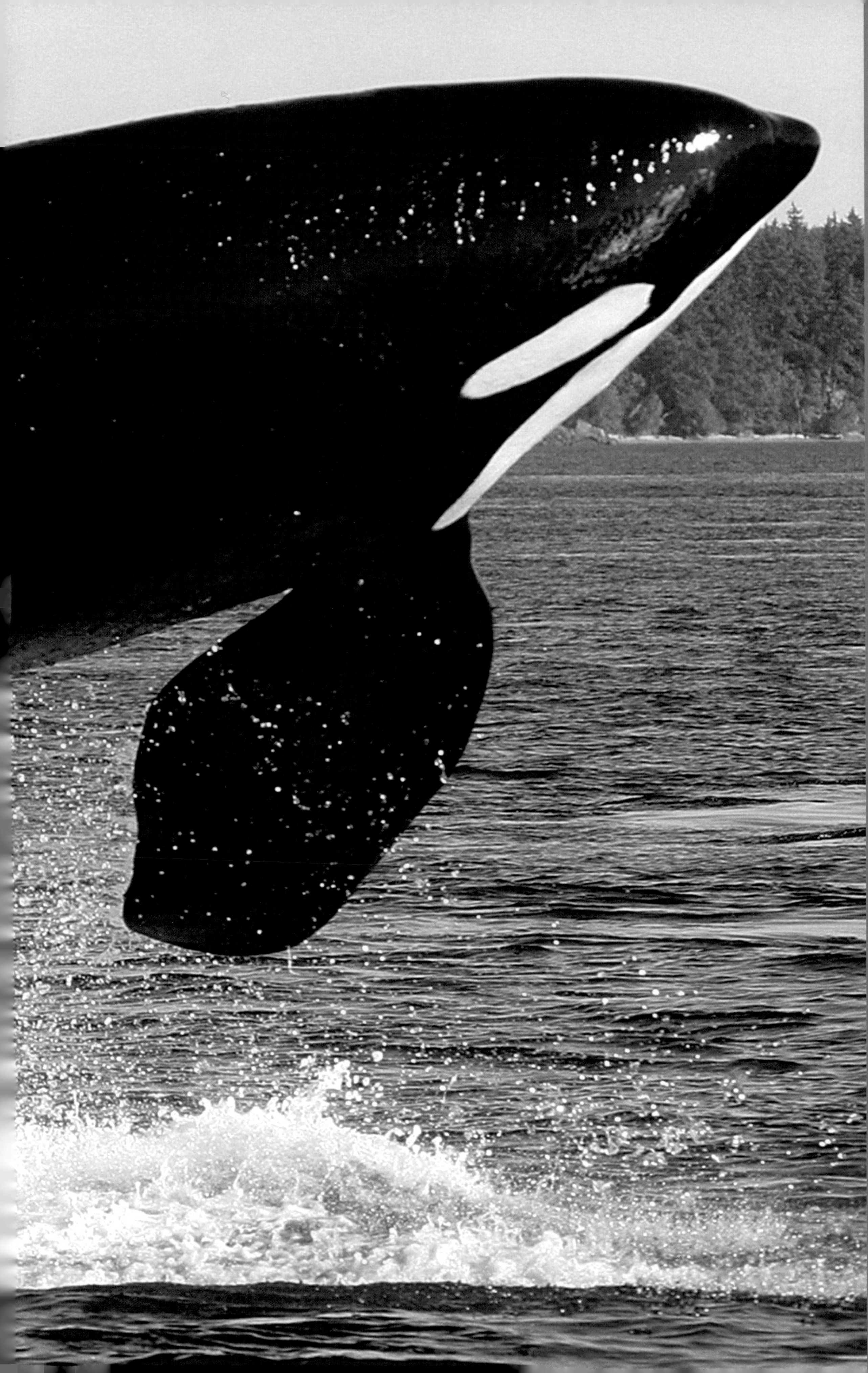

5 The Animal Kingdom

MAMMALS

The mammal class is characterised by three attributes. Firstly, all mammals have glands that enable them to provide milk to feed their offspring. Secondly, mammals are warm-blooded, which means that they try to keep their body temperature constant. Lastly, all mammals have fur or hair.

Take it slow

The slowest mammal in the world is the three-toed sloth. It is so slow that algae are able to grow in its furry coat. This gives the sloth a greenish tint, which provides very useful camouflage in the trees.

Large land mammals

The largest land mammal on Earth is the African elephant, followed by the rhinoceros. The third largest animal is the hippopotamus (*Hippopotamus amphibius*). You can't usually see how big they are, though, as they spend a lot of time in the water.

INTERESTING!

World's fastest animal

Lions, tigers and other big cats are all very fast animals. Speed enables these predators to chase and catch prey. The fastest animal on Earth is the cheetah (*Acinonyx jubatus*) – it can run at speeds of 112–120 km/h (70–75 mph).

SCAN ME
Instructions on page 5

Rodents

The biggest order within the mammal class is that of the rodents. This order includes mice, squirrels, rats and chipmunks. They make up half of the species in the mammal class. A rodent's front teeth never stop growing. If they didn't constantly gnaw on hard materials such as wood, their front teeth would grow right down through their lower jaws. The biggest rodent is the capybara (*Hydrochoerus hydrochaeris*), which can grow to the size of a small dog.

What's it like up there?

The world's tallest mammal is the giraffe (*Giraffa camelopardalis*), which can grow to a height of 4.6–5.5m (15–18ft).

AMAZING!

Duck-billed platypus

The platypus (*Ornithorhynchus anatinus*) is a special mammal. Firstly, the female is one of only two egg-laying mammal species. Secondly, the male is venomous. Male platypuses have a pointy spur on their hind ankles that connects to a venom sac in each leg. A platypus also looks odd – it has a tail like a beaver, a body like an otter, and webbed feet and a beak like a bird.

Flying mammals

Bats are the only mammals that are capable of continued flight. There are over 1,000 different species of bat. *Pteropus* bats, which are also known as flying foxes or fruit bats, are also the largest species of bat in the world.

DID YOU KNOW?

Awesome Mammal Facts

1 TINY, TINY BAT

The smallest mammal in the world is the Kitti's hog-nosed bat (*Craseonycteris thonglongyai*). This bat is 3cm (1¼ in) long and weighs less than 220g (½ lb). It is often called the bumblebee bat.

2 WHAT A CLEVER PIG

Mammals are considered very intelligent animals because of the large size of their brains. Humans are the most intelligent of all mammals, but pigs are also thought to be very smart creatures.

3 BLOOD-SUCKING BATS

There are three species of bat that feed solely on blood. These are called vampire bats. Vampire bats have small, extremely sharp teeth that are capable of piercing an animal's skin without it even knowing.

PRIMATES

Primates are the order of mammals that includes apes, monkeys and humans. There are about 600 species of primate, which can be divided into three main groups – New World monkeys that live in the Americas, Old World monkeys and apes that mostly live in Africa, and the Prosimians that live largely in Madagascar and South-East Asia.

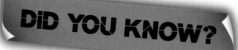

DID YOU KNOW?

Monkey or ape?

Although they are both part of the primate order, there are lots of differences between monkeys and apes. The most obvious one is a tail. Most monkeys have a tail, while apes don't have one at all.

Furthermore, apes can swing from branch to branch as they have a different shoulder-bone structure, which is similar to that of humans. Monkeys cannot swing from branch to branch. Instead, they run along the tops of branches.

Overall, apes are more closely related to humans than monkeys, while monkeys are more similar to other mammals.

Human chimp

The primate that most resembles humans is the chimpanzee. About 95 per cent of the DNA of chimpanzees and humans is the same. Unlike humans, chimpanzees are largely vegetarian. However, male chimpanzees will sometimes hunt and eat meat as well.

Endangered ape

The second largest great ape and the largest tree-living animal is the orang-utan. Male orang-utans are almost twice as big as the females, can weigh up to 77kg (170lb), and have continuously growing cheek pads. The number of orang-utans in the world has dropped dramatically due to the deforestation of tropical rainforests in South-East Asia.

Speedy primate

The patas monkey (*Erythrocebus patas*) lives mostly on the West African savannas. When this species of monkey senses danger, it often throws objects at the predator to avoid getting hurt. If that doesn't work, the monkey has another handy skill – it is the world's fastest primate and can run at speeds of 50 km/h (31 mph).

AMAZING!

World's biggest primate

The largest primate in the world is the gorilla. A male gorilla can grow to about 1.7m (5ft 6in) tall and weigh over 180kg (400lb). The arms of gorillas are longer than their legs and they use them to "knuckle-walk", leaning on their knuckles when they walk on all fours. The hair on the back of older male gorillas turns white, which is why they are also called silverback gorillas.

DID YOU KNOW?

Amazing Primate Facts

1 MONKEY WEE

Male squirrel monkeys (*Saimiri*) sometimes dominate other male or female squirrel monkeys by urinating on them.

2 WORLD'S BIGGEST PRIMATE

Mandrill monkeys (*Mandrillus sphinx*) are the world's largest monkey, with the males growing to a length of 1m (3ft 3in) and weighing about 35kg (77lb).

MARSUPIALS

There are about 334 species of marsupial, 235 species of which live in Australia and New Guinea and 99 species in the Americas. The babies of marsupials are born very early in their development and then develop further in their mother's pouch.

DID YOU KNOW?

Kangaroo species

There are four different species of kangaroo – the red kangaroo (*Macropus rufus*), the eastern grey kangaroo (*M. giganteus*), the western grey kangaroo (*M. fuliginosus*), and the antilopine kangaroo (*M. antilopinus*). Although kangaroos can hop on two legs or walk slowly on all fours, they cannot walk backwards.

Hopping giant

The largest marsupial is the red kangaroo. Male red kangaroos are rusty red in colour and weigh 25–90kg (55–198lb). They measure between 96–160cm (3¼–5¼ ft) in length.

AMAZING!

Sound the alarm!

Kangaroos fight with each other by boxing with their front paws, but will also defend themselves with powerful kicks from their hind legs. When danger approaches, they warn other kangaroos by stamping the ground with their hind feet or thumping it with their tail.

World's smallest marsupial

Measuring 5–6cm (2–2¼ in), the world's smallest marsupial is the long-tailed planigale (*Planigale ingrami*). Planigales can be found in northern Australia.

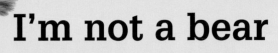

I'm not a bear

Koala bears are not actually bears at all but – you guessed it – a type of marsupial. The closest living relative of the koala (*Phascolarctus cinereus*) is the wombat. Koalas only ever eat eucalyptus leaves and have fingerprints, just like humans.

Tasmanian devils

The closest relative to the Tasmanian devil (*Sarcophilus harrisii*) is the kangaroo. Tasmanian devils are the largest carnivorous (meaning meat-eating) marsupial in the world.

Clever oppossums

Opossums are the only family of marsupials that don't live on one of the Australasian islands. Male opossums are called Jack, females are called Jill, and babies are called Joey – just like other opossum young. When an opossum is threatened, they "play possum", which means that they mimic the appearance and smell of a dead animal.

Little bears

Wombats look rather like little bears. There are two kinds of wombat: bare-nosed and hairy-nosed wombats. Wombats can be extremely aggressive and have been known to attack humans using their strong teeth and claws.

DID YOU KNOW?

Awesome Marsupial Facts

1 POUCH HOME

The term marsupial comes from the word *marsupium*, which means pouch – this is where the mother carries and nurses her young baby.

2 FANCY A DIP?

Wallabies and kangaroos hop around most of the time, but they also quite like to take a dip. No one knows why wallabies and kangaroos swim, but they seem to enjoy it!

3 OLYMPIC JUMP

Kangaroos have strong hind legs and can jump very high – up to three times their own height!

MARINE MAMMALS

Mammals that have adapted to an aquatic life are called marine mammals. Although they live in water, these mammals still have lungs instead of gills like fish. For this reason, they have to come to the surface to breathe. They have extra-large lungs and specially adapted muscles for storing oxygen.

INTERESTING!

20-minute dive

There are seven species of sea lion and all of these species are endangered. They are very good swimmers and can stay under water for up to 20 minutes. Baby sea lions (which are known as pups) do not know how to swim when they are first born. They learn to swim on their own when they are a couple of weeks old.

Largest seal

Elephant seals are rather funny-looking seals, with a trunk-like inflatable snout. They are the largest of all the seals – the males can be over 6m (20ft) long and weigh up to 4,000kg (8,800lb). When the breeding season starts, male elephant seals define and defend their territories. They collect a harem of 40–50 females.

Tooth walk

The Latin name for the walrus is *Odobenus rosmarus*, which means tooth-walking seahorse. When a walrus uses its huge tusks to pull its massive body out of the water onto the pack ice, it looks as if it is walking on its tusks, hence the name.

Largest animal on Earth

The blue whale (*Balaenoptera musculus*), the world's largest living animal, is an aquatic mammal. The largest blue whale reached a length of 33.5–35m (110–115ft) and weighed over 117,934kg (260,000lb)!

Killer whale

One of the most amazing aquatic mammals is the orca or killer whale (*Orcinus orca*), which is actually a part of the dolphin family. Killer whales are known as the "wolves of the sea" because of their pack-like hunting techniques.

Sleepy whale

Whales never fall asleep completely because they regularly need to go up to the surface of the sea for air. If they didn't swim up to breathe, they would suffocate or drown.

Dolphin echo

Dolphins are believed to be very intelligent creatures. They have excellent eyesight and hearing, as well as the ability to use echo location to find the exact whereabouts of objects and food.

Whale or unicorn?

The narwhal (*Monodon monoceros*) is a whale species with a long ivory tusk, measuring 2–3m (6½–10ft), which extends from the upper left side of its jaw. For this reason, narwhals are known as the "unicorns of the sea". They have been known to make some of the deepest dives of any marine mammal – up to 1,524m (5,000ft) deep – in search of food.

FISH

Fish are a class of aquatic vertebrate. What makes them different from other animals is a combination of three factors. Firstly, they use gills to breathe under water; secondly, they have fins that they use to move around in water; and, lastly, they can only live in water.

Tropical fish

As the name suggests, tropical fish live in tropical areas of the world. Most of these fish live on the coral reefs. Tropical fish are often brightly coloured and so make popular pets.

DID YOU KNOW?

Fish species

Scientists believe that there are more than 30,000 different species of fish in the world. That is more than all the species of amphibians, reptiles, birds and mammals put together.

Age rings

When a fish grows, it doesn't add new scales to its body. The scales simply grow with the fish. Rings form on the scales as the fish grows, which can be used to work out the age of a fish in much the same way as you can deduce the age of a tree from the rings in its trunk.

AMAZING!

Lungfish

Lungfish are one of the few fish that have both gills and lungs. Because of their lungs they are able to live out of water for several years. Lungfish burrow under the earth and take in air with their lungs through a built-in breathing tube that extends up to the surface of the ground.

Human teeth

Although fangtooth fish are only tiny, they have teeth that are about the same size as a human being's.

School of fish

A school, or group of fish, may contain millions of fish. The fish use their eyes and a lateral line to hold their place in the school. The lateral line is a row of pores that runs along the fish's side from head to tail. Special hairs in the pores sense changes in water pressure from the movements of other fish or predators. Only bony fish can swim in schools. The fish in the middle of the school control the movement of the school.

Horse or fish?

Although the name suggests that this creature is some sort of underwater horse, seahorses are, in fact, fish. They are the only fish that swim upright, but are not very good swimmers. Seahorses would rather rest in one place. Unlike with other animals, male seahorses become pregnant and give birth to the young.

DID YOU KNOW?

Amazing Fish Facts

1 FOUR-EYED FISH

Anablep fish have four eyes so they can look under and above water at the same time.

2 FISH HEAVEN

Tropical fish are one of the most popular pets in America.

3 ANCIENT FISH

The oldest known fish ever recorded was a species of lungfish – it reached an age of 65 years old!

DEADLY FISH

The Earth's waters can be very dangerous. Among the thousands of fish species are some very dangerous fish indeed. These include fish that will attack and/or eat us, fish that may poison us with their stings, and fish that can bite or electrocute us. So, don't go too deep!

What a lot of teeth

Sharks have 40–45 teeth with up to seven rows of replacement teeth behind them. Sharks will go through more than 30,000 teeth in a lifetime.

Shark tales

There are about 350 different types of sharks, but most of them are not dangerous at all. The biggest shark, the whale shark (*Rhincodon typus*), can be as big as a bus, but only eats plankton. More than 90 per cent of people attacked by sharks will survive. In reality, more people are killed each year by bee stings than by sharks. Strangely, sharks are more likely to attack men than women.

Ancient fish

The first sharks lived 400 million years ago, which is 200 million years before the first dinosaurs.

Dangerous sharks

Although it is rare, sharks do sometimes attack people. The three most dangerous sharks are the great white (*Carcharodon carcharias*), the tiger shark (*Galeocerdo cuvier*) and the bull shark (*Carcharhinus leucas*), with the 7-m (23-ft) long great white shark leading the list for the highest number of attacks on humans.

Lionfish

Also known as dragon fish or Turkey fish, lionfish have long, poisonous spines that are deadly to many sea creatures. However, with the right medical treatment, a lionfish sting will only cause severe pain, headaches and vomiting in humans.

Electric shock

The electric eel (*Electrophorus electricus*) is capable of generating a shock of 500 volts to shock its prey or scare off predators. That is enough to harm humans and large mammals very seriously.

Look where you're going!

Hammerhead sharks have eyes on the outer edges of their distinctive hammer-shaped nose. This gives them a vertical 360-degree view, but also means that they have a big blind spot right in front of its nose.

Piranhas

Piranhas have very sharp teeth and can easily tear off flesh from their prey. When underfed, they even turn into cannibals.

Most poisonous fish

Stonefish are the most poisonous fish in the world. Their sting can cause shock, paralysis and even death if not treated within a few hours.

Stingrays

Most rays are harmless, but stingrays have one or more barbs on their tails that they use to defend themselves. The barb contains a painful venom, but the sting is only fatal if there is no medical attention available.

AMPHIBIANS

Amphibious means "having two lives", and refers to the two different life stages of amphibians such as frogs and toads. Starting life in the water with gills and fins like fish, amphibious creatures then develop lungs and legs so that they are able to survive on land. Not all amphibians live totally on land, however, and will always prefer to reside in damp areas.

Hitching a ride

The Surinam toad (*Pipa pipa*), which is also known as the star-fingered toad, has a unique and rather weird reproduction technique. After laying her eggs, the female toad carries them on her back. To keep them safe, her skin grows around the eggs, forming little holes for them and making the skin on her back look like a sponge. When the eggs hatch, the young toads climb out of her back.

AWESOME FACT!

Massive frog

The world's largest frog is the Goliath frog (*Conraua goliath*). It can grow up to 90cm (3ft) long when stretched out and weighs about 3.2kg (7lb). These frogs live in African rainforests and are highly endangered. They can live for up to 15 years, but don't breed easily or survive well in captivity.

Smallest amphibian

With a length of only 7.7mm (⅓ in), *Paedophryne amauensis* is the world's smallest amphibian. It lives in New Guinea and is also the world's smallest vertebrate.

Baby belly

Gastric brooding frogs from Australia, which are now thought to be extinct, swallow their fertilized eggs. These unusual frogs raise their tadpoles in their tummy until they have developed into frogs. The froglets then come hopping out of their parents' mouths.

Axolotl salamander

One of the few salamanders that retains its larval features is the axolotl (*Ambystoma mexicanum*). This salamander keeps its external gills and tadpole-like fins, but can grow up to 30cm (12in) long. Axolotls live in lakes around Mexico City, where they are considered a delicacy. This means that the axolotl is now an endangered species.

Toxin attack

Many newts produce toxins in their skin secretions, which they use as a defence mechanism against predators. The rough-skinned newt (*Taricha granulosa*) of the Pacific Northwest produces enough toxins to kill an adult human.

Largest amphibian

The largest amphibian in the world is the Chinese giant salamander (*Andrias davidianus*). They can grow as long as 1.8m (6ft).

What's a caecilian?

There is a group of slender-bodied, limbless amphibians called caecilians. They are closer to reptiles such as earthworms and snakes in appearance, but are a fairly unknown part of the amphibian group.

DID YOU KNOW?

Awesome Amphibian Facts

1 GOLDEN POISON

The golden poison arrow (or dart) frog (*Phyllobates terribilis*) has enough poison in its system to kill 20 humans.

2 MARCHING ARMY

A group of frogs is called an army of frogs.

3 THIRSTY SKIN

Frogs don't drink with their mouths; instead, they absorb water through their skin.

4 LOTS OF FROGS

90 per cent of all amphibians are frogs.

REPTILES

Reptiles are cold-blooded animals that have lungs. Most reptiles live on land. They lay hard-shelled eggs and their bodies are covered with scales. These scales can be bony and hard like a crocodile's skin or soft and smooth like a snake's.

Tuataras

This reptile group used to be spread across the New Zealand mainland, but there are only two species of tuatara remaining, as rodents and humans have nearly driven them to extinction. The two living species are the Cook Strait tuatara (*Sphenodon punctatus*) and the Brother's Island tuatara (*Sphenodon guntheri*).

Four reptile groups

Reptiles can be divided in four main groups: turtles, squamata (lizards and snakes), crocodilians, and tuataras (these are lizard-like in appearance, but their skulls are not joined).

Hot and cold

In some species of turtle, the temperature determines if an egg will develop into a male or female. Low temperatures result in a male turtle, while high temperatures produce a female one.

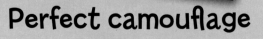

AWESOME FACT

Perfect camouflage

The chameleon is a master of disguise because it has the ability to change colour. Nerves cause areas of colour in the skin to spread out or become concentrated into tiny dots. The chameleon uses this ability to get close its prey without being seen or to hide from predators. It also uses its colours to communicate with other chameleons. Fighting male chameleons can display very bright colour schemes to impress each other.

SCAN ME
Instructions on page 5

Largest lizard

The Komodo dragon (*Varanus komodoensis*) is the world's largest lizard. It lives on the South-East Asian islands and grows up to 3m (10ft) long.

Poisonous lizards

There are only two poisonous lizards in the world – the Gila monster (*Heloderma suspectum*) and the Mexican beaded lizard (*Heloderma horridum*). The poison is made in glands in the lizards' lower jaws. Both lizards live in south-western North America.

World's most dangerous snakes

Saw-scaled carpet vipers, which live in Africa and Asia, are the world's most dangerous snakes. They are extremely aggressive and their poison can kill humans.

Fastest snake

The black mamba (*Dendroaspis polylepis*), which lives in Africa, can wriggle along at up to 11 km/h (7 mph). This makes it the fastest-moving snake on land.

DID YOU KNOW?

Awesome Reptilian Facts

1 SALTY SEA TURTLES

Sea turtles have special glands which help remove the salt from sea water so that they can drink it.

2 BIGGEST TURTLE

The world's largest turtle is the leatherback turtle (*Dermochelys coriacea*). It grows up to 1.6m (5ft 3in) in length and weighs up to 360kg (794lb).

3 TAIL ESCAPE

Many lizards can shed their tail in order to escape from a predator. Don't worry, the tail grows back again.

CROCODILES AND ALLIGATORS

These reptiles are extremely dangerous and, with their powerful jaws and sharp teeth, are on top of their food chain. They have streamlined bodies and strong legs, which means that they can move very fast in water and on land, making them one of the most dangerous animals to humans.

DID YOU KNOW?

Alligator or crocodile?

Although they are quite similar, you can spot differences between alligators and crocodiles. Alligators have a wide, broad nose, while crocodiles usually have a narrow nose. A crocodile also has teeth sticking out of its snout when its mouth is closed.

There are only two types of alligator: the American alligator (*Alligator mississippiensis*) and the Chinese alligator (*Alligator sinensis*). As you might guess, they are found in China and the United States, mostly in Florida and Louisiana. The crocodile is more widely spread, being found in the tropical regions of Asia, America, Africa and Australia. There is a salt-water species of crocodile as well.

Aren't you a dinosaur?

The crocodile has looked the same since the time of the dinosaurs. They are about 200 million years old.

Crocodile skin

The skin of a crocodile's belly is regarded as one of the finest for making leather goods and is treasured for its durability and softness. It is a sign of status for a lot of tribes.

AMAZING!

Big crocs!

The Nile crocodile (*Crocodylus niloticus*) grows up to 6m (20ft) long, making it one of the world's largest crocodiles. However, the world's biggest crocodile i the salt-water crocodile (*Crocodylus porosus*), which is found in the waters between India and Australia.

Egg sitting

The female crocodile lays about 30 or more eggs in a pit she digs for a nest. She covers the eggs with earth or sand, and then carefully guards the nest for about three months. When the eggs hatch out, she gently carries the hatching young in her mouth down to the water. The little ones have to find their own food, but their mother will react to their distress calls. The father crocodile is less parental and sees his young as a food source.

AWESOME FACT!

Cooling off

Crocodiles sit on the banks of rivers with their mouths open. That's not a sign of aggression – they are just trying to cool off, as they sweat through their mouths.

Breathtaking achievement

Alligators and crocodiles can hold their breath under water for nearly an hour.

Crocodile tears

When people display fake sadness, we say that they are crying "crocodile tears". The term originates from the myth that reptiles weep when they are eating humans. They do wipe their eyes when they're feeding, but only because their eyes bubble and froth when eating.

Grinder stone

rocodiles have 24 sharp teeth that are designed to grasp and crush, but not to chew. They swallow stones to grind food inside their stomachs.

BIRDS

Animals with feathers, a beak and wings that lay hard-shelled eggs are called birds. Birds are the only animals that can be found on every single continent on Earth. Although all birds have wings, they can't always fly.

Hollow bones

Birds have hollow bones. This makes them lighter, so they can take off and fly.

World's largest bird

The ostrich (*Struthio camelus*) is the largest bird in the world and can also run faster than any other bird, reaching speeds of 97 km/h (60 mph).

Smallest bird

The bee hummingbird (*Mellisuga helenae*), which lives in Cuba, is the world's smallest bird. It is only 5cm (2in) long.

Kiwi nose

Kiwis are the only birds that have nostrils at the tip of their beak. Whereas other birds hunt by sight or hearing, the kiwi uses its beaky nostrils to sniff out food at night.

Migration

Around 20 per cent of bird species migrate long distances each year. They migrate from the colder northern areas to the warmer southern ones. They fly in a V-formation in order to save energy on these long journeys. Well-known bird species that migrate in a V-formation are geese.

AMAZING!

Largest wingspan

The wandering albatross (*Diomedea exulans*) has the largest wingspan of any living bird. As a result, it is an excellent glider and is able to stay in the air without beating its wings for several hours. The largest known specimen had a wingspan of 3.6m (12ft). An albatross can also sleep while flying.

Tern migration

The Arctic tern (*Sterna paradisaea*) makes the longest migration of any bird. Each year it makes a journey of 35,000km (21,748 miles). The terns nest in the Arctic during the summer and travel to areas near Antarctica to escape the cold winter.

Prison break

The female Great Indian hornbill (*Buceros bicornis*) lays her eggs in a hole in a tree – and then stays there. The male bird seals up the hole, leaving just a narrow slit through which he passes food to the female. The female stays in the hole until the chicks are a few months old, and then she breaks out of her prison nest and helps the male with feeding duties.

Massive penguin

The Emperor penguin (*Aptenodytes forsteri*) is the biggest penguin in the world. It stands about 115cm (45in) tall. Like other penguins, it cannot fly, but is a very good swimmer. Emperor penguins are the only birds that can breed in the cold Antarctic winter.

Polar birds

There are only a few animals that can survive the harsh climate of Antarctica. Penguins are one of them. There are 18 species of penguin and they all live on or around Antarctica.

BIRDS OF PREY

This bird group includes hawks, eagles, osprey, condors, vultures, kestrels, owls and many other species. There are about 307 species of birds of prey (or raptors) in the group. All these birds are skilled hunters with superb eyesight, strong legs and talons, and a sharp, hooked bill.

Fastest bird

The peregrine falcon (*Falco peregrinus*) circles above a victim before making a fast dive and killing its prey on impact. During the dive, the falcon can reach speeds of 320 km/h (199 mph), which is faster than any other bird.

AMAZING!

Biggest nest

Bald eagles (*Haliaeetus leucocephalus*) make a nest – known as an eyrie – that is the biggest nest made by any bird. It can be 5.5m (18ft) deep. The eagles use the nest again and again, adding more nesting material each year to make it bigger.

Vulture diet

The diet of vultures consists mainly of carrion (or dead meat), which they detect from the air. Vultures don't find carrion on the day it is killed, but usually on the second or third day once it has begun to rot. The decaying carcass gives off a strong odour that helps vultures locate their next meal.

Fishy prey

Ospreys (*Pandion haliaetus*) eat fish and have become experts at fishing due to their long legs and sharp talons. They dive into water to catch fish and have a special waxy layer on their feathers to protect them.

Chewy stomach

Birds don't have teeth to chew their food because, otherwise, they would be too heavy to fly. Instead, birds "chew" their food inside a part of their stomach called a gizzard. The gizzard has strong muscles that grind the food against a rough inner surface in order to break it down.

Sibling rivalry

Most birds of prey lay between one and six eggs, but not all at the same time. They wait a day or two after each egg before laying the next. The first chick to hatch is bigger than the others and may actually kill its younger siblings if food is scarce.

Three eyelids

The eyes of birds of prey are so important for their survival that they have developed three eyelids. The third one is partially see-through, which allows birds of prey to protect their eyes while attacking prey and still have some sight.

DID YOU KNOW?

Amazing Bird of Prey Facts

1 OWL FEATHERS

Owls have soft-edged flight feathers that allow them to fly almost silently – so they can sneak up on unsuspecting prey.

2 LARGEST BIRD OF PREY

The largest bird of prey is the Andean condor (*Vultur gryphus*), at 110cm (43in) long. It has a wingspan of 3m (10ft).

3 HAWK'S VIEW

Hawks have excellent hearing and eyesight. Their vision is eight times greater than ours.

CRAWLING INSECTS

Insects represent about 90 per cent of all life forms on Earth. Lots of people think of insects as pests, but they are actually very useful to the world because they produce wax, honey and silk, and also pollinate plants.

Insect anatomy

All insects have three body parts – the head, thorax and abdomen. They have six jointed legs and two antennae.

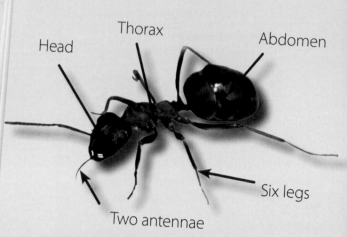

Head

Thorax

Abdomen

Six legs

Two antennae

Insect skeleton

Insects have an exoskeleton, which contains sense organs for detecting light, sound, temperature, wind, pressure and smell.

DID YOU KNOW?

Weightlifting champions

Ants are tiny but, compared with humans, they are extremely strong. One single ant can lift 100 times its own body weight.

Brainy insect

The brain of a cockroach is located within its body, so, even if it were to lose its head, the cockroach could survive for nine days before finally dying of hunger.

Beetle family

The largest group of insects that has been identified are the beetles. One out of every five living species is a beetle.

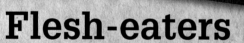

Flesh-eaters

Dermestes maculatus or flesh-eating beetles are only tiny, but have an important job to do. They strip animal carcasses down to the bone. Without this little beetle the world would be full of rotting animal carcasses.

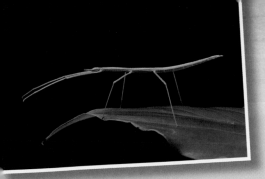

Big eater

The desert locust (*Schistocerca gregaria)* is the world's most destructive insect. It can eat its own body weight in food in a day. People normally eat their own body weight in about half a year.

Camouflage stick

One of the best-camouflaged insects are walking sticks. Strangely, they can regenerate lost limbs. Female walking sticks can also reproduce by themselves, but will only produce other females.

Most toxic insect

The Maricopa harvester ant (*Pogonomyrmex maricopa*) is the world's most poisonous insect. Its sting causes severe pain to humans, but 12 of its stings can easily kill a 2kg (4½ lb) rat.

Termite mounds

African termite mounds can be 12m (40ft) high and use an intricate system of ventilation shafts to control the temperature inside.

Dung beetle

The dung beetle feeds on animal waste. They especially love the dung of herbivores and some even use it to lay their eggs in.

DID YOU KNOW?

Awesome Insect Facts

1 LARGEST INSECT

Giant weta are the world's largest insects, measuring up to 10cm (4in) in length.

2 ANT STOMACH

An ant has two stomachs: one to store food for itself and the other to store food to share with other ants.

3 HEAD TURNER

There is only one insect in the world that can turn its head – the praying mantis.

FLYING INSECTS

Insects are the only invertebrates that have evolved the power of flight. Not all insects can fly, however, and even having wings doesn't always mean an insect can fly long distances. Some insects also only have wings for a certain phase in their life.

Traveller bees

Honeybees have to travel an average of 69,202km (43,000 miles) to collect enough nectar to make one pound of honey. Honeybees have hairs on their eyeballs so that they can work out speed and direction during their journey.

Killer bees

Bees kill more people each year than do snakes or sharks. Killer bees live in colonies of around 80,000 bees – they are quick to get excited and attack in swarms.

Tiny wasp

The world's smallest winged insect is the Tanzanian parasitic wasp. It is smaller than the eye of a housefly.

Toothy grin

The average mosquito has 47 teeth!

Short lifespan

Dragonflies only live for 24 hours and have as many as 30,000 lenses in each eye. Dragonflies are the world's fastest insects, flying at speeds of 80–96 km/h (50–60 mph).

AWESOME FACT!

Lightning bugs

Lightning bugs or fireflies are not real flies; they are actually beetles. Male lightning bugs glow to attract females. Each species of the 2,000 different lightning bugs has its own pattern of light flashing.

Wing ears

Night butterflies have ears on their wings so that they can avoid being eaten by a bat.

Spider meal

Tarantula wasps paralyse tarantula spiders and then lay a single egg on the still-living spider. When the egg hatches out, the wasp larva feeds on the spider.

Tsetse flies

Bloodsucking tsetse flies, which live in Africa, cause a lot of sicknesses and death among people in Africa.

Blood-suckers

Mosquitoes can be a real pain, but only female mosquitoes drink blood in order to obtain the nutrients they need to produce eggs.

Painful bite

Horseflies are one of the world's largest flies. A bite from a horsefly is painful because the fly cuts a hole into the skin to soak up blood. Luckily, only female horseflies bite!

Human bot fly

The torsalo or human bot fly (*Dermatobia hominis*) lays an egg on a mosquito. When the mosquito feeds on a human, the egg hatches and the larva crawls onto the human and burrows into the skin to feed. After a few weeks the larva crawls out of the skin as a fly.

Bleeding knees

The ladybird doesn't have many enemies. They have a bitter-tasting blood that is disliked by most animals and, when threatened, a ladybird will bleed from its knees.

Massive moth

The Atlas moth (*Attacus atlas*) is one of the world's largest moths, with a wingspan of over 20cm (8in).

ARACHNIDS

This group includes spiders, scorpions, ticks and mites. Arachnids have eight legs and their bodies have two parts: a head and an abdomen. They do not have feelers. Scorpions and spiders prey on other insects. Thankfully, not all scorpions and only a few spiders are dangerous to humans.

Most poisonous spider

Brazilian wandering spiders are the most venomous spiders in the world. However, in spite of their strong toxin, there have only been a few fatal incidents with people.

Scared of spiders

When you have an abnormal fear of spiders, it is called arachnophobia.

AWESOME FACT!

Hungry female

After mating lots of spider females eat the male. Some male spiders take some food along when mating in the hope of not being eaten.

Spitting spiders

Spitting spiders have a very interesting way of catching their prey. They have poison glands in their head and spitting glands in their abdomen. When ready to catch prey, they push their front and back segments together and spit poisonous silk at the insect to kill it.

DID YOU KNOW?

Large spiders

Tarantula spiders are by far the largest spiders in the world – their size and hairy legs make many people shiver. The largest species of tarantula is the Goliath bird eater (*Theraphosa blondi*), which is found in the rainforests of South America. It has a legspan of up to 30cm (12in).

AMAZING!

Ticks

Ticks can't jump or fly, but instead they crawl onto the legs of their victim or jump from a high object. Ticks are attracted to a host by body heat, odour from the skin, and carbon dioxide.

Sick children

Studies show that children who are continually exposed to dust-mite faecal material are more likely to develop asthma, allergies and eczema.

DID YOU KNOW?

Bed pets

Mites thrive in warm, dark, moist places. They feed on dead-skin flakes (known as dander), so your bed is an ideal environment for them. They will happily live in sheets, duvets, mattresses and pillows – these can be infested with thousands of mites.

Poisonous

There are about 2,000 species of scorpions, about 40 to 50 of which have a poison that is strong enough to kill people.

Survivors

Scorpions can survive without food for up to a year and without water for two months. They do this by slowing down their metabolism.

Scorpling dinner

The scorpion mother will carry her baby scorpions (called scorplings) on her back until she sheds her skin for the first time after the birth. Scorplings are in danger of being eaten by their hungry mother.

MOLLUSCS

Molluscs are a group of animals that have no skeleton. The word "mollusc" means "soft", which is why they were given their name. Most species of mollusc live in water, but some slugs and snails have adapted to live on land. Many species have a shell made from calcium to protect them from predators.

Hidden pearls

Pearls come from molluscs. Any mollusc with a shell can make pearls, although the most common pearl-makers are oysters. Pearls are made when a foreign object such as dirt gets inside the shell of a mollusc by accident. To protect itself, the creature covers the intruding object with the same material that its shell is made from, which is a mineral known as nacre. The mollusc continues covering the object with multiple layers of nacre until a pearl is eventually formed.

DID YOU KNOW?

Mollusc classification

Molluscs can be divided into eight groups, including bivalves such as mussels and clams, gastropods like snails and slugs, and cephalopods such as squid and octopus.

Ancient fossils

Scientists have found snail fossils that date from millions of years ago. Snails are considered to be one of the world's oldest-known species of animal. They have been around for more than 600 million years.

AWESOME FACT!

Hermaphrodite

Snails are hermaphroditic, which means that they are both male and female. However, a snail will always try to mate with another snail instead of fertilizing its own eggs.

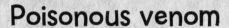

Ink defence

Squid release a cloud of dark ink when being attacked or if they feel threatened.

Giant clam

The giant clam (*Tridacna gigas*) is the world's largest bivalve mollusc and considered a delicacy in Japan. It has a lifespan of over 100 years and weighs more than 200kg (441lb).

Poisonous venom

Octopuses are true hunters. They change colour to merge with their surroundings and wait for unsuspecting prey to pass by. When a prey animal is close enough, the octopus grabs it with its long arms and secretes a nerve poison that stuns the prey. Octopus venom is poisonous and can be fatal to people as well, especially from species of the blue-ringed octopus (*Hapalochlaena*).

DID YOU KNOW?

Amazing Mollusc Facts

1 BLUE BLOOD

The octopus has three hearts and blue blood.

2 SAY THAT AGAIN

Did you know that snails have no sense of hearing?

3 DON'T BE NOSEY!

Slugs have four noses … that would explain their snotty appearance!

Largest invertebrate

Giant squid (*Architeuthis*) are the world's largest type of invertebrate. They can reach lengths of 9–16m (30–52ft).

FOOD

All animals need to eat. They either eat plants, other animals, or organisms like bacteria and fungi. Some foods such as plants are difficult to digest, while other foods like prey animals can be difficult to catch. Animals are perfectly adapted to their main food source and the way in which they obtain it.

Migration

Some animals live in herds and have to travel in order to find enough of their plant food, as well as the best types of food. These herds travel long distances to find fresh grass and this travelling is called migration. Wildebeest, for example, migrate to the savannah every November at the start of the rainy season and then to the forests in May when the dry season starts.

INTERESTING!

Herbivores

Animals that live largely on a diet of plants or algae are called herbivores. Some herbivores eat a wide variety of plants, while others eat one particular type of plant – pandas, for example, will only eat bamboo. Plants are difficult to digest and not very nutritious, so herbivores often have to eat lots of them.

Carnivorous teeth

There are many different types of carnivore, but they all have one feature in common – their teeth. All carnivores have four large scissor teeth for slicing through meat. As the mouth closes, the teeth slide past each other like blades.

Carnivores

Carnivores are animals that eat other animals. Not only are large mammals such as tigers, lions and wolves carnivorous, but so too are insect-eaters such as birds and fish-eaters like grizzly bears.

Underground storage

Burying beetles eat dead animals. When a beetle finds a carcass, it digs a hole to preserve the food and then digs a nest next to the hole so that its larvae can feed on the carcass easily.

Clever monkey

The Japanese macaque (*Macaca fuscata*), a species of monkey, is very hygienic when it comes to food. It washes its food in the sea before eating it. The salt in the water also gives the food a little seasoning.

Bird kebab

The northern shrike (*Lanius excubitor*) is a songbird that is mostly found in southern Canada and the northern United States. It captures insects or other small vertebrates and then skewers them onto thorns, spiny stalks or even barbed-wire fences. This clever bird can then eat its food in little portions from the stalks.

It can even eat a poisonous animal, slicing it open and waiting for a few days for the poison to dry out before eating it.

AMAZING!

Omnivores

When animals are adapted to eat plants and animals, we call them omnivores. Humans are the best-known omnivores, but a lot of other animals are also omnivorous. Animals such as badgers, squirrels, skunks, pigs and some bears are all omnivores.

SLEEP

Sleep is the time when the body rests. There is a reduction in physical activity and a decreased response to outside stimuli. Sleep comes in many forms: sometimes an animal only needs a power nap lasting a few seconds, while other animals sleep or hibernate for the winter season.

INTERESTING!

Nocturnal animals

Not all animals sleep at night like humans. Instead, they sleep or are very lazy during the day and then come alive and hunt at night. We call these animals nocturnal. Examples of nocturnal animals include foxes, bats, owls and badgers.

Why are animals nocturnal?

Most animals are **diurnal** (meaning they are active in the day), so there is a lot of competition for food during the day. Therefore, some animals have adapted to hunt at night and have become **nocturnal**. Animals also became nocturnal to avoid the heat of the day.

Best night vision

Owls have the best night vision of all nocturnal animals. They are able to spot a mouse on a football pitch lit by just a single candle. However, owls are long-sighted, which means that they find it difficult to see things right in front of their eyes.

Marmots

Alpine marmots (*Marmota marmota*) hibernate for eight months of the year. They spend the other four months producing babies and preparing for hibernation.

Sleepy hamsters

Lots of hamsters are kept as pets. However, hamsters are nocturnal which makes them quite an odd choice for a pet! They sleep all day and then become active during the night when you go to bed.

AMAZING!

Long lemur sleep

The fat-tailed lemur (*Cheirogaleus medius*) is the only known animal in the Tropics that hibernates. It will stay in its tree hole for seven months of the year.

Hibernation

Most animals struggle to find enough food, such as insects or green plants, in the winter. Some animals solve this problem by hibernating. Hibernation is a deep sleep in which an animal's temperature drops and its heartbeat and breathing slow down so that it doesn't use much energy. The animal will prepare for hibernation by eating extra food and storing this as body fat. Hibernating animals include frogs, turtles, polar bears and lots of insects.

Science & Technology

6

THE WORLD OF ATOMS

Atoms are the basic building blocks of all matter in the Universe. Atoms are made up of particles called protons, neutrons and electrons. There are trillions and trillions of different atoms, which create different elements such as hydrogen and carbon depending on how many electrons, protons and neutrons the atom contains.

Ernest Rutherford

In 1919 the physicist Ernest Rutherford was the first person to break down atoms into nuclei and electrons. He split a nitrogen atom into hydrogen and oxygen. He was also the man who discovered the existence of protons.

Electrons

An electron is a negatively charged particle that spins around the nucleus of an atom, attracted by the positive charge of the protons in the nucleus. Electrons spin around the nucleus so fast that scientist can never be completely sure of where the electrons are located. Electrons are about 1,800 times smaller than protons and neutrons.

What is a nucleus?

There is a nucleus at the centre of every atom, which contains positively charged protons and neutrons that don't have any charge. The number of neutrons affects the mass as well as the radioactivity of the atom.

Hydrogen atoms

The hydrogen atom is unique in that it only has a single proton and no neutron in its nucleus. This makes it the lightest known element.

What is a molecule?

Two or more atoms joined together create a molecule. Different types of atom joined together are called compounds. For example, water (H_2O) is made up of two hydrogen atoms and one oxygen atom. A molecule is the smallest part of a substance that can exist on its own.

What is a bond?

Molecules are held together by forces known as chemical bonds. There are two different types of bond: **covalent bonds** and **ionic bonds**. We call a bond covalent when atoms share their electrons. An ionic bond is when an atom donates an electron to another atom.

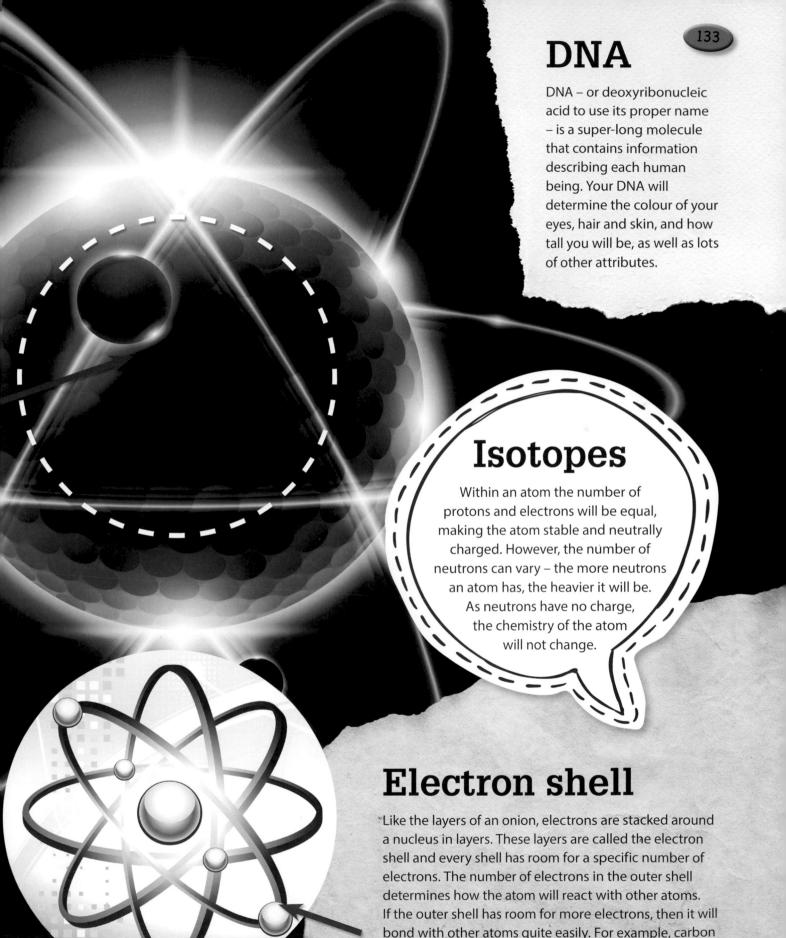

DNA

DNA – or deoxyribonucleic acid to use its proper name – is a super-long molecule that contains information describing each human being. Your DNA will determine the colour of your eyes, hair and skin, and how tall you will be, as well as lots of other attributes.

Isotopes

Within an atom the number of protons and electrons will be equal, making the atom stable and neutrally charged. However, the number of neutrons can vary – the more neutrons an atom has, the heavier it will be. As neutrons have no charge, the chemistry of the atom will not change.

Electron shell

Like the layers of an onion, electrons are stacked around a nucleus in layers. These layers are called the electron shell and every shell has room for a specific number of electrons. The number of electrons in the outer shell determines how the atom will react with other atoms. If the outer shell has room for more electrons, then it will bond with other atoms quite easily. For example, carbon (C) has four electrons in its outer shell and room for four more, so it bonds easily with other atoms.

THE PERIODIC TABLE

An element is a pure substance that is made from a single type of atom. There are currently 118 known elements. Of these, only 94 are thought to exist naturally on Earth; the others are man-made. The elements are listed in the Periodic Table according to the structure of their atoms.

Other non-metals

The elements that are considered to be non-metals are hydrogen, carbon, nitrogen, phosphorus, oxygen, sulphur and selenium. They are all either gases or solids, with the gases nitrogen and oxygen making up most of the Earth's atmosphere.

Mendeleev

The Periodic Table was originally compiled by the Russian chemist and inventor Dmitri Mendeleev in 1968.

Element families

Some elements have similar properties and are therefore grouped together. In general, they have the same colour in the Periodic Table. Examples of family groups are the noble gases, alkali metals and halogens.

Marie Curie

Born Manya Sklodowska, in Poland, Marie Curie discovered two new elements while working in Paris, in France. One of these elements was the extremely dangerous radium. Marie named the other element polonium after her homeland. She and her husband, Pierre, also came up with the term radioactivity in order to describe those elements that emit strong rays.

Alkali metals

The alkali metals all have one electron in their outer shell and are therefore extremely reactive. The alkali metals are lithium, sodium, potassium, rubidium, caesium and francium. These are all soft, shiny metals.

Snap!

The elements found on Earth and Mars are exactly the same.

Missing letter

The only letter that does not appear in the Periodic Table is the letter J.

Noble gases

The atoms of noble gases all have an outer shell that is full of electrons. For this reason they do not react with other elements. When an electric current is passed through noble gases, they glow with bright colours. The noble gases are helium, neon, argon, krypton, xenon and radon.

Halogens

Fluorine, chlorine, bromine, iodine and astatine make up the halogen family. They form acids when combined with hydrogen, and are all fairly toxic and highly reactive. All halogens have two atoms in their pure form, which are also known as di-atomic molecules.

Atomic numbers

Each element has a unique atomic number, called the atomic number, which tells us the number of protons in each atom. For example, hydrogen has one proton, so it has an atomic number of 1, while gold has 79 protons in each atom and therefore has an atomic number of 79. Each element in its standard state will have the same number of electrons, too.

Periodic Table

Element	Symbol	Atomic mass	Atomic number
Hydrogen	H	1.008	1
Helium	He	4.003	2
Lithium	Li	6.941	3
Beryllium	Be	9.012	4
Sodium	Na	22.99	11
Magnesium	Mg	24.31	12
Potassium	K	39.10	19
Calcium	Ca	40.08	20
Scandium	Sc	44.96	21
Titanium	Ti	47.87	22
Vanadium	V	50.94	23
Chromium	Cr	52.00	24
Manganese	Mn	54.94	25
Iron	Fe	55.84	26
Cobalt	Co	58.93	27
Nickel	Ni	58.69	28
Copper	Cu	63.55	29
Zinc	Zn	65.39	30
Gallium	Ga	69.72	31
Germanium	Ge	72.63	32
Arsenic	As	74.92	33
Selenium	Se	78.96	34
Bromine	Br	79.90	35
Krypton	Kr	83.80	36
Rubidium	Rb	85.47	37
Strontium	Sr	87.62	38
Yttrium	Y	88.91	39
Zirconium	Zr	91.22	40
Niobium	Nb	92.91	41
Molybdenum	Mo	95.94	42
Technetium	Tc	[98]	43
Ruthenium	Ru	101.07	44
Rhodium	Rh	102.91	45
Palladium	Pd	106.42	46
Silver	Ag	107.87	47
Cadmium	Cd	112.41	48
Indium	In	114.82	49
Tin	Sn	118.71	50
Antimony	Sb	121.76	51
Tellurium	Te	127.60	52
Iodine	I	126.90	53
Xenon	Xe	131.29	54
Caesium	Cs	132.91	55
Barium	Ba	137.33	56
Hafnium	Hf	178.49	72
Tantalum	Ta	180.95	73
Tungsten	W	183.84	74
Rhenium	Re	186.21	75
Osmium	Os	190.23	76
Iridium	Ir	192.22	77
Platinum	Pt	195.08	78
Gold	Au	196.97	79
Mercury	Hg	200.59	80
Thallium	Tl	204.38	81
Lead	Pb	207.2	82
Bismuth	Bi	208.98	83
Polonium	Po	[209]	84
Astatine	At	[210]	85
Radon	Rn	[222]	86
Francium	Fr	[223]	87
Radium	Ra	[226]	88
Aluminium	Al	26.98	13
Silicon	Si	28.09	14
Phosphorus	P	30.97	15
Sulfur	S	32.07	16
Chlorine	Cl	35.45	17
Argon	Ar	39.95	18
Carbon	C	12.01	6
Nitrogen	N	14.01	7
Oxygen	O	16.00	8
Fluorine	F	19.00	9
Neon	Ne	20.18	10
Boron	B	10.81	5
Rutherfordium	Rf	[267]	104
Dubnium	Db	[268]	105
Seaborgium	Sg	[269]	106
Bohrium	Bh	[270]	107
Hassium	Hs	[269]	108
Meitnerium	Mt	[278]	109
Darmstadtium	Ds	[281]	110
Roentgenium	Rg	[281]	111
Copernicium	Cn	[285]	112
Ununtrium	Uut	[286]	113
Flerovium	Fl	[289]	114
Ununpentium	Uup	[289]	115
Livermorium	Lv	[293]	116
Ununseptium	Uus	[294]	117
Ununoctium	Uuo	[294]	118

Lanthanides

Element	Symbol	Atomic mass	Atomic number
Lanthanum	La	138.91	57
Cerium	Ce	140.12	58
Praseodymium	Pr	140.91	59
Neodymium	Nd	144.24	60
Promethium	Pm	[145]	61
Samarium	Sm	150.36	62
Europium	Eu	151.96	63
Gadolinium	Gd	157.25	64
Terbium	Tb	158.93	65
Dysprosium	Dy	162.50	66
Holmium	Ho	164.93	67
Erbium	Er	167.26	68
Thulium	Tm	168.93	69
Ytterbium	Yb	173.04	70
Lutetium	Lu	174.97	71

Actinides

Element	Symbol	Atomic mass	Atomic number
Actinium	Ac	[227]	89
Thorium	Th	232.04	90
Protactinium	Pa	231.04	91
Uranium	U	238.03	92
Neptunium	Np	[237]	93
Plutonium	Pu	[244]	94
Americium	Am	[243]	95
Curium	Cm	[247]	96
Berkelium	Bk	[247]	97
Californium	Cf	[251]	98
Einsteinium	Es	[252]	99
Fermium	Fm	[257]	100
Mendelevium	Md	[258]	101
Nobelium	No	[259]	102
Lawrencium	Lr	[262]	103

SOLIDS, LIQUIDS AND GASES

Solid

Liquid

Gas

Substances can exist in three different states on Earth: solid, liquid or gas. For example, a solid is the wood that your chair is made out of, the water you drink is a liquid, while the air you breathe is a gas.

Liquids

In a liquid state, the particles move around a little; therefore, liquids can flow into any shape, while their volume stays the same. Water is the most common liquid on Earth. Did you know about 60 per cent of the human body is made of water?

Freezing point

Freezing is when substances turn from a liquid to a solid state. This is the minimum temperature of the liquid. Most liquids reduce in volume in their solid state. Water freezes at 0°C (32°F).

Solids

A solid substance is created when its particles are locked together and have a definite shape and volume. Water is one of the few substances that will expand when it is in its solid form – which is called ice. Most other substances reach their smallest volume when they are in their solid state.

Gases

Gaseous substances do not have a definite shape or volume. The particles move around all over the place, which enables the gas to expand and contract depending on pressure and temperature.

Boiling point

When a liquid reaches its maximum temperature, it boils. After that point it turns into a gaseous state. Liquids all have their own boiling point – water, for example, has a boiling point of 100°C (212°F).

That's so cold

The lowest freezing point of any metal is that of mercury which freezes at -39°C (-38.2°F). Helium has the lowest freezing point of any substance, at -268.9°C (-452.02°F).

Highest melting point

The metal with the highest melting temperature is Tungsten, which melts at 3,410°C (6,170°F). The highest known melting point for any substance belongs to carbon, which will melt at a temperature of 3,527°C (6,380.6°F).

Lowest boiling point

There is less pressure higher up in the mountains and this has an effect on the boiling point of liquids. On top of Mount Everest, for example, the boiling point of water decreases to 71°C (159.8°F) at 8,848m (29,029ft).

Plasma

A fourth state of matter exists, but this only occurs when a gas becomes extremely hot. Extreme heat makes the atoms and molecules collide, and the electrons are ripped free. This process happens inside the Sun, in other stars and also in lightning.

Changing states

Substances can change state from a solid to a liquid or a liquid to a gas, for example, by heating, cooling, or boosting or reducing the energy of their particles. For instance, you can heat up an ice cube until it melts and becomes water, while you can boil water until it evaporates and takes the form of water vapour.

Melting point

Melting is the opposite of freezing. This means that solids will turn liquid at their melting point, which is the maximum temperature of the solid. Lead melts at a temperature of 327.5°C (621.5°F).

ENERGY

Energy comes in many forms, including chemical energy, kinetic energy, nuclear energy, renewable energy, electrical energy, heat energy, sound energy and light. Different types of energy can also be converted from one form to another.

Electrical energy

Electricity is the presence of an electric charge. An electrical current only flows in a closed circuit and will flow as long as there is a difference in charge between two points in that circuit. The difference is called a potential and is measured in volts. The electric current is measured in amperes (amps).

Hydo-electric power

Water can also be used to generate electricity. As water runs along a river, it spins the turbines of a generator. Another way to produce electricity with water is by building a hydro-electric dam. This allows the amount of water running through the dam to be controlled, depending on the weather and how much electricity is needed. The more water flowing through the dam, the more electricity will be created.

Batteries use a Direct Current (DC).

War of the currents

In the 1800s there was a battle between Thomas Edison and Nikola Tesla. Edison helped invent Direct Current (DC), which means that the electric current flows in the same direction at all times. Tesla won the war with his Alternating Current (AC), which lets the current constantly change direction. The Alternating Current is also safer and can be used over longer distances. The electricity in our homes is all AC, while battery-operated appliances are DC.

Lightning power

Lightning is a huge flash of energy that is caused by a build-up of electricity in the clouds. The electrical spark may pass from one cloud to another or from a cloud to the ground. Some buildings have lightning conductors to draw the electrical charge away from the clouds.

Solar power

The Sun is one of the most powerful sources of energy. The sunlight that shines on the Earth in just one hour could supply the world with enough energy for a whole year. However, we are not using more solar power because solar-power systems are very expensive and different wiring is required in our houses.

Wind farms

Special windmills are used to generate electricity. When the wind turns the blades of one of these windmills, it spins a turbine inside a small generator to produce electricity. A site with several windmills is called a wind farm. The bigger the wind turbine, the more electricity it can produce.

AMAZING!

Conductors

When an electric current travels through a material or substance, we call that material or substance a conductor. Metals like copper and silver make the best conductors. That's why electric wires are made out of copper. Water is also a very good electrical conductor.

Renewable energy

When energy is made from resources that cannot be used up, such as wind, water or sunshine, we call it renewable energy. This form of energy is also known as "clean energy" or "green power" because it doesn't pollute the air or water.

THE WORLD OF FORCES

Forces make something or someone move with a pushing and pulling motion. Forces are all around us and always work in pairs. Forces can be invisible, as in the case of gravity, but there are also visible forces such as a push or shove.

Gravity

The invisible force of attraction between every object in the Universe is called gravity. It keeps the Planets orbiting the Sun and it keeps us firmly on Earth. The strength of the gravity depends on the mass of the objects and the distance between the objects. Mars is smaller and has less mass than Earth, and so it has less gravity. Someone weighing 45kg (100lb) on Earth would only weigh 17kg (38lb) on Mars.

Sir Isaac Newton's three physical laws

Scientist Sir Isaac Newton discovered Three Laws of Motion in 1687, which provided three simple rules for understanding the movement of objects in the Universe.

2. Acceleration

Newton's Second Law of Motion states that the larger the force and the lighter the object, the quicker it will gain speed – this is called acceleration.

1. Momentum

Put simply, when a force makes something else move, the object will keep moving until another force makes it stop. This is how momentum is described in Newton's First Law of Motion. When two objects collide, their combined momentum stays the same if nothing else interferes. So, if one object loses its momentum, then this has to be passed on to another object, making it move instead. This knock-on effect can be seen in action in a fun piece of apparatus called Newton's Cradle.

3. Push and pull

Newton's Third Law of Motion states that for every action there is an equal and opposite reaction. This means that whenever something moves, there is a balance of forces pushing in the opposite direction.

Terminal velocity

When skydivers fall out of a plane, their speed accelerates first. While they are accelerating, the friction in the air grows until the gravity and the friction are equal. From this point, the speed will stay constant – this is called the terminal velocity. For a skydiver, this speed is around 160.9 km/h (100 mph).

Friction

Friction is the word we use to describe the force created when two things rub together. Friction slows things down and also makes them hot because their momentum or movement is converted into heat.

DID YOU KNOW?

Amazing Facts About Forces

1 MEASURE THE POWER

Forces can be measured using a force meter. The force is measured in Newton (N).

2 STILL STANDING

Did you know that it is very difficult to stand up without friction?

3 FALLING APPLES

It is believed that Sir Isaac Newton worked out his Theory of Gravity when an apple fell from a tree and hit him on the head.

MAGNETISM

When the electrons in a molecule spin in the same direction, a unique and invisible force is created, which we call magnetism. The arrangement of the atoms creates two poles in a magnet: a north-seeking pole and a south-seeking pole.

Magnetic fields

The magnetic force in a magnet runs from its north pole to the south pole, so creating a magnetic field around the magnet. The strength of the magnetic field decreases the further away from the magnet you go. A magnetic field is measured in Teslas after the scientist Nikola Tesla.

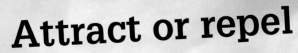

Attract or repel

The two north poles and two south poles of two magnets will repel each other. Only the two opposite poles will attract.

AMAZING!

Compass

A compass contains a tiny bar magnet that always points to the North Pole. You can make your own simple compass by attaching a bar magnet to a piece of wood. Then, float the wood in a bowl of water. The magnet's north pole will turn and point to the Earth's North Pole.

DID YOU KNOW?

Magnetisation

To make your own magnet, take a piece of iron and rub it on another magnet. This process is called magnetisation and will turn any suitable piece of metal into a magnet.

Metal magnets

Due to the arrangement of their electrons, metals such as iron, nickel and cobalt make strong magnets. They are also highly attracted to other magnets. However, most metals, including copper, silver, gold, magnesium, platinum and aluminium, are not attracted to magnets.

What are lodestones?

Before people were able to make steel magnets, they found that lumps of certain types of rock called lodestones would repel or attract each other or bits of iron. This happens because they contain iron oxide.

AWESOME FACT!

The biggest magnet

Planet Earth is a huge magnet with a magnetic force created by its iron inner core and liquid iron outer core. The North and South Poles behave like the poles of a magnet. Animals like whales and birds use the Earth's Poles to find their way when they migrate. The Earth's magnetic field also protects us from the Sun's solar winds and radiation.

Ancient Greece and China

Magnetism was discovered and used over 800 years ago in Ancient Greece and China. These ancient civilizations even made their own compasses.

Magnetic cows

Dairy farmers and vets feed or insert magnets into cows to prevent disease. When cows graze, they often swallow things such as bits of wire and nails left in the field. These objects can cause inflammation and irritation. The cow will lose its appetite and will not be able to produce milk. The little magnet inside the cow, however, can prevent this happening by pulling all the iron objects together, so keeping the cow healthy.

LIGHT AND SOUND

Light is very important for life on Earth. It prevents the Earth from being a dark, cold planet and helps plants make food through photosynthesis. Light travels in a wave-like manner, just like sound. Sound starts with a vibration and reaches your ears as a vibration that travels through the air in waves.

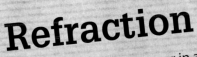

Refraction

Light travels in tiny waves or in a straight line called a ray. However, when light passes through a transparent material such as water or glass, it bends or turns. Because of their different wavelengths, each colour in the spectrum bends at a different angle and the incoming white light is split into different colours. This process is called refraction. Lenses in a pair of spectacles use refraction to help us see better, as does the lens in a telescope when we want to see things that are far away.

Wavelengths

The distance between the top of a wave and the next wave is called the wavelength. The smaller the wavelength, the higher the sound will be. Low sounds will have a large wavelength. Every colour in the light spectrum has its own wavelength, too – red has the longest wave and violet has the shortest.

Ear to the ground

Sometimes you can hear the sound of a large animal such as a galloping horse before you can actually see it. This is because sound waves travel much faster through the ground than they do through the air.

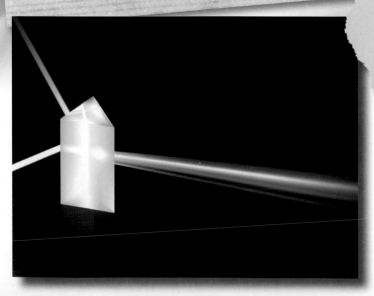

The Doppler Effect

If you are standing still and a car drives past you, the frequency of the sound will change as the car passes. This is called the Doppler Effect. The sound pitch will be higher as the car is coming towards you. The sound pitch will become lower as the car moves away from you. The sound is not actually changing, but the speed of the car coming towards you is making the sound reach your ear quicker.

Fastest thing in the universe

Light travels at 300,000km (186,411 miles) per second. It is the only speed in the Universe that never changes. This speed makes light the fastest-moving thing in the whole Universe.

AWESOME FACT!

Sound barrier

Sound travels at a speed of 343 metres per second (768 mph). When aeroplanes go faster than the speed of sound, they break the sound barrier. When they pass through the speed of sound, an aeroplane sheds water drops that have condensed on the plane, creating a cool-looking white halo.

Breaking the sound barrier also creates a **sonic boom**. This is a loud noise like an explosion that is generated from a number of sound waves being forced together as the plane is travelling faster than sound.

Why is the sky blue?

As light from the Sun passes through the Earth's atmosphere, it is scattered in all directions by gases and tiny particles in the air. The blue light is scattered about more than the red, yellow, orange and green light because it has a shorter and smaller wavelength. This is what makes the sky look blue on a clear day.

A RAINBOW OF COLOUR

Light helps us to see different colours. Every colour has its own wavelength and the objects around us will absorb some of these wavelengths, but reflect others. So, for example, when an object absorbs all of the wavelengths except for the red one, we see that object as red.

Blue

Looking at the colour blue can make the human body produce calming chemicals, but blue can also be cold and depressing. People are more productive in blue rooms, while studies show that weightlifters can lift heavier weights in gyms that are painted blue.

Green

Green symbolises nature and is the most popular choice of colour when people are decorating their homes. This is because it can have a healing effect on us. Green is also calming, just like blue. Brides in the Middle Ages wore green to symbolise fertility.

Yellow

Yellow is a colour for attention-seekers. Although yellow is regarded as an optimistic colour, more people lose their temper and babies will cry more often in a yellow room. On the plus side, yellow can enhance concentration and speed up metabolic rates.

Primary and secondary colours

Red, blue and yellow are primary colours which cannot be made by mixing other colours together. Green, orange and purple are secondary colours that can be made by mixing the primary colours. For example, blue and yellow make green; red and blue make purple; and red and yellow make orange.

Black and white

Black and white are not real colours. We see an object as black because it absorbs all of the colour wavelengths. In contrast, a white object absorbs none of the colour wavelengths and reflects them instead, and so we see the object as white.

White

Brides often wear white, which is a colour of innocence and purity. Doctors and nurses wear white to imply sterility.

Black

Black is the colour of authority and power. Quite often, villains in stories wear black because it has such a powerful and negative effect.

Purple

The colour purple stands for royalty, luxury, wealth and sophistication. It's also very feminine and romantic. Purple is a very rare colour in nature. A purple room is said to help children develop their imagination.

Red

Red is the most commonly used colour in flags. It is also frequently used in food packaging because supermarkets believe it makes people feel hungry – and then they will buy more food!

DID YOU KNOW?

Awesome Facts About Colours

1 CAR COLOURS

The most popular colour of car is white in America, black in Europe, and silver in Asia.

2 SAILFISH

Sailfish can change colour instantly in order to confuse their prey during an attack.

3 BLACK CATS

The Ancient Egyptians believed that black cats have divine power. Nowadays, we often think that black cats will bring us bad luck.

BACTERIA AND VIRUSES

Bacteria are tiny organisms that are everywhere around us. We have to use a microscope to see them. They are single-celled micro-organisms that are made from cells similar to those of plants. Viruses are just like bacteria – they are very small, too, but have to invade a host in order to multiply.

Body bacteria

We have many good bacteria in our bodies that help us to digest food. Other bacteria help our immune systems to fight off the bad bacteria that can make us sick.

AMAZING!

Sickening for something

Most bacteria are harmless, but some can make us sick. These bacteria are called pathogens and can cause illnesses such as food poisoning, pneumonia and tetanus in animals and humans. Plants can also be affected by bacterial infections.

Medication needed?

There are two different types of infection: **bacterial infections** and **viral infections**. A doctor can prescribe antibiotics to kill the bacteria that cause a bacterial infection. Viral infections such as the common cold, influenza, chickenpox, measles or mumps cannot be treated with antibiotics and so you have to wait for your immune system to fight them off.

Helpful vaccinations

A vaccination can protect you against some nasty diseases. When you are vaccinated against certain types of infection, a little bit of the disease you are being vaccinated against is injected into your body. Scientists have cleverly developed vaccinations that contain just enough for your immune system to be able fight off the disease without you becoming ill. Once your body has fought off a virus, it is impossible for that virus to take hold in your body again.

Herd immunity

People who are vaccinated even protect those who have not been vaccinated because they don't provide a place for the disease to multiply and spread from. This is called herd immunity. Vaccination programmes can be so effective that some diseases no longer exist. Smallpox was once a deadly disease, but has been largely eliminated by herd immunity.

Useful food bacteria

Bacteria are used in the production of some types of food. Without the help of bacteria, for example, we wouldn't have cheese, yoghurt, pickles or soy sauce.

ROBOTS

Machines that can work on their own automatically are called robots. The simplest type of robot is a mechanical toy that is programmed to perform a series of actions, usually with no real function. Some robots are simple, remote-controlled devices, while the most complex robots have artificial intelligence, which is the ability to make decisions, solve problems and learn.

First robot

In the 5th century BC Archytas of Tarentum built a mechanical bird driven by a jet of steam or compressed air – this was probably the first ever robot.

Artificial Intelligence

Artificial Intelligence (AI) will change things radically in the near future. While scientists have yet to explore the full potential of AI, it is already making life a little easier for us. There are AI robots that can do the vacuuming and manoeuvre around obstacles like furniture, stairs and even pets. In the near future we will probably see AI used for driverless transport, cleaning the environment, more extreme space exploration, privacy and safety, and household chores. We might even create a trans-human species, incorporating technology into the human body that will eliminate disabilities, slow down the ageing process, and maybe even prevent death altogether.

ASIMO

Japanese motor manufacturer Sony developed ASIMO, which is a very special robot. It even made a world tour, showing off its walking, running and dancing skills. After being updated, ASIMO could detect and avoid oncoming people, carry a tray and push a trolley.

AMAZING!

Space robots

Robots are as important to space travellers as they are to soldiers in wars. Exploring places that are too dangerous to send human astronauts, robot spacecraft and surface vehicles, which are called rovers, are often used instead.

War robots

Robots are very useful in wars because they can enter dangerous situations without risking human lives. They can find and dispose of bombs and landmines while the operator stays at a safe distance.

AIBO

AIBO is a robot made by Sony that behaves and moves like a dog. Robots that simulate animals are a vital step forward in the development of future robots.

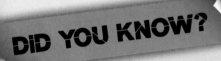

DID YOU KNOW?

Industrial robots

Factories have become much more efficient with the help of industrial robots. These robots usually take the form of mechanical, computer-controlled arms or they are used to perform tasks that are too dangerous for people. Robots are also great at doing jobs that call for repeated actions because they are more accurate than a human being – they also don't need breaks or holidays!

Surgeon helpers

Surgeon robots make it possible to perform surgery through an incision of just 1cm (½ in) wide. By inserting minuscule instruments and a viewer called an endoscope, the surgeon can see the operation site on a screen and move the robot's instruments by remote control.

TRANSPORT BY RAIL AND ROAD

It all started with the invention of the wheel more than 6,000 years ago in Mesopotamia. Since then many forms of road and rail transport have been invented, including carts, carriages, bicycles, trains and cars. Early trains were powered by steam engine and most cars run on petrol, but we are now looking for more eco-friendly fuels.

Bicycles

After walking, the bicycle is the world's most common form of transport. Bikes are cheap to buy and run, and they do not create any pollution.

Speedy travel

The fastest way to travel over land is by train. Some superfast trains can reach speeds of up to 300 km/h (186 mph).

Stop – emergency!

Trains usually have four braking systems available but, even in a full emergency, it can take a train 1.6km (1 mile) or more to stop. This means that if the train driver can see you, it is already too late for him to stop and avoid hitting you.

STOP

DID YOU KNOW?

That's a big fine!

The largest speeding fine ever given was for £643,000 (US$ 99,000) to a Swedish man, who was driving 290 km/h (180 mph) in Switzerland. Unfortunately, Switzerland has no fixed penalties for speeding; the fine is based on the speed and the salary of the driver.

First trains

George Stephenson invented a steam train – Stephenson's *Rocket* – in 1829, which was first used to transport the public from 1830. These early trains ran on coal and steam, but now trains can run on electricity and sometimes even solar energy.

Travelling underground

Using underground transport systems in big cities such as London, New York and Paris is the fastest method of travel. The first system of underground rail transport was opened in London in 1863 – the London Underground. New York's underground rail network has a total 468 stations, making it the world's biggest underground railway. The London Underground is often referred to as the Tube, while Paris has its Metro and New York has the famous New York Subway.

Musical journey

The first car radio was invented in 1929. Before then long journeys must have been very boring. Over 90 per cent of drivers admit to singing along with the radio behind the wheel.

Bike nation

The Netherlands is a true bike nation. Indeed, 30 per cent of all trips in the Netherlands are made by bicycle. Seven out of eight Dutch people over the age of 15 own a bike. They even build special roads and traffic lights for bicycles!

DID YOU KNOW?

Amazing Transport Facts

1 RECYCLING

Cars are the most recycled consumer product in the world.

2 TWO WEEKS' WAIT

On average human beings spend two weeks of their lives waiting for traffic lights to change.

TRANSPORT BY AIR AND WATER

For thousands of years, ships and boats transported people and cargo to different places all over the world. Although massive cargo ships still carry huge quantities of goods around the globe, most people choose to travel long distances by aeroplane nowadays.

World's longest ship

The container ship, the *Maersk E-Class*, is the world's longest cargo ship, measuring over 397m (1,300ft) in length. However, it will be replaced this year by the 400-m (1,312-ft) long *Maersk Triple E-Class*.

First air travellers

In September 1983 a sheep, a duck and a cockerel were the first air travellers in a hot-air balloon built by Joseph and Etienne Montgolfier. Later that year, their balloon carried two men across Paris.

Egyptian shipping

All major Ancient Egyptian cities were built on the banks of the River Nile. Therefore, their main method of transport was by boat. The Egyptians' first boats were made out of a plant called papyrus, which is the same material that they used to make paper. They also thought a boat was needed in the afterlife, so a small model of a boat would be buried with a dead person.

Cruise ships

Cruise ships are among the tallest ships in the world. They carry thousands of people, keeping them entertained with lots of restaurants, swimming pools, clubs, cinemas and shops. The world's largest cruise ships are *Allure of the Seas* and *Oasis of the Seas*, which both cruise in the Caribbean.

Archimedes' Principle

How boats float is explained in the Archimedes' Principle. This explains how an object displaces some of the water when it is lowered into the water. The principle is exactly the same as the water level rising when you get into a bath. When the amount of water that is being displaced is equal to the weight of the object, then it will float.

Top 10 busiest ports

Seven out of the ten busiest ports in the world are located in China. The third one is in Singapore and the tenth is in South Korea. The fourth busiest – and also largest – port is Rotterdam in the Netherlands. It is the only non-Asian port in the Top 10.

Safest flight

Helicopters or choppers are the safest way to travel through the air. The rotor blades allow a helicopter to slow down, stop, fly sideways and even fly backwards. If the engine of a helicopter stops, the rotor blades continue to spin so that often the machine can slowly land without crashing to the ground.

Wright brothers

Orville and Wilbur Wright made the first flight in an aeroplane called the *Flyer* in 1903. The flight lasted for 12 seconds and they flew for 36.6m (120ft).

MUSIC

Music is one of the oldest of the performing arts. There are many different genres of music, including classical music, jazz and pop. Different generations and cultures enjoy different types of music, but most people find it can be very expressive, influencing their mood and making them want to dance.

The Beatles record sales: 600 million

Elvis Presley record sales: 500 million

Michael Jackson record sales: 250 million

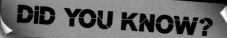

DID YOU KNOW?

Musical genres

Every period in history has its own music style. Young people usually promote a new type of music. Classical music was one of the first types of music. In the 1950s Rock 'n' Roll music started in America with popular artists like Elvis Presley. In the 1970s there was disco, which eventually changed into the dance music of the 1990s. Rap music has become one of the biggest forms of music of the last couple of decades, outselling most other musical forms.

AMAZING!

Beethoven

German composer Ludwig van Beethoven (1770–1827) was one of the world's greatest composers of classical music. He was known for his bad temper and scruffy appearance (the police even arrested him thinking that he was a tramp). Beethoven started performing when he was only seven years old. Sadly, towards the end of his life, he lost his hearing and couldn't hear his own music anymore.

Best-selling artists

Some artists sell millions of albums and singles, even after they die or stop making music. Here are the five best-selling artists (their active years are in brackets):

1. The Beatles (1960–1974)

2. Elvis Presley (1954–1977)

3. Michael Jackson (1964–2009)

4. Madonna (1979–present day)

5. Led Zeppelin (1968–1980)

Madonna record sales: 300 million

Led Zeppelin record sales: 200 million

Musical instruments

To enjoy music you need musical instruments. There are many different types of musical instrument, which are divided into five main groups:

Wind instruments

require a person to blow into the instrument. The shorter the air column, the higher the pitch of the note produced.

Examples Flute, clarinet, oboe, harmonica, piccolo, bagpipes and accordion.

Percussion instruments

require a person to strike or beat its surface to produce sound.

Examples Drums, xylophone, tambourine, cymbals, triangle and djembe.

String instruments

produce sounds with the help of strings. The pitch of the note depends on the length and thickness of the strings.

Examples Violin, cello, harp, guitar, viola and ukulele.

Brass instruments

are a shiny version of wind instruments. While wind instruments have set a length of air column, these can be adjusted in brass instruments while playing to make different sounds.

Examples Trumpet, tuba, saxophone, trombone and bazooka.

Electronic instruments

are the newest group of musical instruments and still developing. Most of these electronic instruments are designed to produce the sounds of other instruments, but in a more user-friendly way.

Examples Keyboards, sampler and synthesizer.

DANCE

People dance to celebrate good times, as part of a ritual, or just to have fun. You can dance on your own, with a partner, or with a group of people. Although it may be for different reasons, people of all ages enjoy dancing as a means of self-expression. It's also a great way to keep fit and healthy!

SCAN ME
Instructions on page 5

Let's dance!

Every type of music has its own dance style. Dancing styles have changed over the years. In the past, dancing was more formal and people weren't allowed to touch each other. Today, ballroom dances are based on contact and interaction between dancers. The favourite dance form for little girls is often ballet, while might boys prefer street dance, which is part of the hip-hop culture along with rap music.

Flamenco

Reflecting its flamboyant culture, the flamenco is a very popular dance in Spain. Between 1869 and 1910 flamenco grew in popularity – this was known as the Golden Age of Flamenco. Women usually wear red, black, navy blue or white dresses with lots of layers of ruffles and high heels. They wear their hair in a bun and often place a rose behind their ear. Men wear black or red tuxedo undershirts with stretchy pants for ease of movement.

Viennese waltz

When it was first performed the Viennese waltz shocked upper class society because of how the dancing partners held each other – it was as if they were in an embrace!

The waltz developed from an Austrian dance known as the *Ländler*. The music of a famous Austrian composer called Strauss popularised a faster version of the waltz – the Viennese Waltz. The waltz is known for the sweeping turns with which the couple gracefully move around the floor.

Hopak

This Cossack dance, which is also known as *Gopak* or *Hopak*, is a Ukrainian dance. It is mostly performed as a solitary concert dance by ensembles and also incorporated into larger artistic works such as operas and ballets. It is often popularly referred to as the National Dance of Ukraine.

African dance

Most African tribes dance to celebrate weddings, harvests and other happy times. These dances involve a lot of hip action and the dancers stamp their feet out of time.

Tap dancing

An early form of tap dance was popular at the start of the 19th century among African-American slaves. They used tap dancing to maintain the history of rhythms and beats that had been passed down through generations. The slaves used their feet to tap the beat because they weren't allowed to play drums or other instruments from Africa.

Charleston

In the roaring 1920s, a popular dance was the Charleston, which was created by the black community in Charleston. It was banned from various halls, as it was considered too scandalous and exuberant. Women wore short dresses and men wore suits.

LITERATURE AND THEATRE

In the past, long before the development of writing, people told stories to explain what was happening in the world and to educate each other. Quite often, stories were told simply as a means of entertainment. People then started writing stories down so they did not forget them. Some stories were acted out in theatres so that the story-teller could reach more people.

Fiction or non-fiction

All literature can be divided into two main groups – fiction and non-fiction. In fictional books, the author creates imaginary events, settings and characters. Non-fiction is based on facts. One of the most famous pieces of non-fiction is the *Diary of Anne Frank* (1947) in which Anne describes her life as a Jewish girl growing up in Amsterdam during the Second World War.

Literary genres

Fiction and non-fiction books can be further divided into genres. Fiction contains genres such as action-adventure, fantasy, science fiction, mystery and romance. Non-fiction genres include journals, diaries, documentaries, biographies, journalistic articles and user manuals.

INTERESTING!

Children's books

Some books are written especially for children. Authors may specialise in writing stories for a defined age group or write for children in general. The Victorian author Charles Dickens's stories, including *Oliver Twist* (1838) and *A Christmas Carol* (1843), were never intended for children, but are often read by children today.

Medieval theatres

In the medieval period theatre buildings were not permitted throughout Europe. Travelling players, who were often known as minstrels, performed on the streets along with jugglers, puppeteers, acrobats and storytellers. Christians thought this kind of entertainment was a sin.

William Shakespeare

One of the world's most well-known playwrights is William Shakespeare (1564–1616). He was born in Stratford-upon-Avon, in England, and grew up in Tudor times. He moved to London to become an actor, but became one of the most famous writers of all time.

AMAZING!

Ancient Greek entertainment

Theatre originated in Ancient Greece and artists would perform songs, dances and plays in open-air theatres called amphitheatres. The actors received a warm welcome everywhere they went.

Poetry

Stories can be told in different forms. In poetry the words follow a rhythm. This could be a certain number of syllables in a line, rhyming words or the first letters forming a message.

DID YOU KNOW?

Awesome Literary Facts

1 TIMELESS THEATRE

Shakespeare's plays, written more than 400 years ago, are still performed all over the world today. Some of his plays include *Hamlet*, *Macbeth*, *Romeo and Juliet*, *Othello* and *A Midsummer Night's Dream*.

2 TODAY'S FAMOUS AUTHORS

Well-known authors of children's books today include Roald Dahl, J.K. Rowling, Eric Carle and Beatrix Potter. Even famous people, such as the singer Madonna and the comedian David Walliams, have written children's books.

PHOTOGRAPHY AND FILM

Cameras are used to record things. They either capture a moment in a photograph or an event in a movie clip. All cameras used to capture these photographs and movies on film (sheets of plastic coated with light-sensitive chemicals). Today, photographs and movies are usually shot digitally and saved on microchips.

DID YOU KNOW?

Camera obscura

One of the first camera-like devices was the *camera obscura*. It used a pinhole or lens to project an image of an upside-down scene onto a viewing surface. Real cameras were developed in the 1830s. In those days a camera was a big box, rather than a device you could easily carry around with you and fit into your pocket.

Hidden mothers

In Victorian times it could take hours to take a photograph. Adults can sit still for a while, but it was very difficult for most children to sit still for such a long time. To help them do this, Victorian mothers often had to hold them in place for the shot while hidden under a sheet dressed up as a chair!

AMAZING!

Sepia photographs

With green blood, three hearts and the ability to change colour instantly, the cuttlefish – a member of the same family as octopus and squid – is an amazing animal. Cuttlefish ink was used by early photographic artists to make photographs more durable. The ink gave the photographs a reddish-brown glow and they became known as sepia images.

Computer movies

Since the 1970s film-makers have used special effects. First they used models, but now computers create most effects. Film-makers can fake explosions on the computer and bring characters to life using motion capture technology. Today, animated films are made entirely on computers, too.

BLAM

ZAP!

Film cameras

In 1888 the roll of film was invented, which made cameras much cheaper and smaller. The image was captured on the film as a negative, which means that all of the light areas appeared dark on the film and vice versa. To create a positive print, light is shone through the negative image onto a piece of light-sensitive paper.

Feature films

The first films were very short. Later on, longer films called features were produced which did not have any sound. They were sometimes accompanied by live music and were always in black and white.

DID YOU KNOW?

Amazing Film Facts

1 SILENT STAR

One of the most famous silent movie stars was Charlie Chaplin.

2 THE FIRST TALKIE

In 1927 *The Jazz Singer* became the first major film to have dialogue.

3 THE WIZARD OF OZ

One of the first films to use colour was *The Wizard of Oz*, which was released in 1939.

DIFFERENT MEDIA

The different ways in which people communicate information to a large audience are known as the media. This information can be written, spoken, printed or in a digital form. The first media were newspapers and magazines, followed by radio and television. Digital media is the newest form of media.

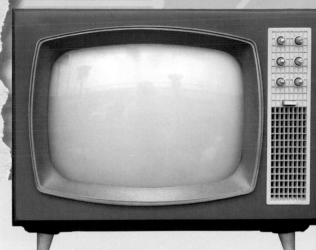

Television

The first television sets went on sale in the late 1920s. At first the picture only appeared in black and white, but colour televisions became widespread in the 1970s. The remote controller became common in the 1980s.

AMAZING!

Magazines

The Gentleman's Magazine, first published in 1731 in London, is considered to have been the first general-interest magazine. Edward Cave, the editor, used the name *Sylvanus Urban* and was the first to use the word "magazine". Magazines cover current events or may focus on a specific subject such as movies, music, fashion, gardening, dogs, etc.

DID YOU KNOW?

Newspapers

Newspapers can be weekly or daily, bringing people news and stories from all over the world. They also contain advertising. China leads the world in newspaper consumption, as the people there read 93.5 million newspapers every day. However, because of the time it takes to print the copies, newspapers are considered old news. This has forced newspaper companies to publish their material online as well.

Radio

Radio began as wireless telegraphy in 1866 and went on to develop into an important means of communication during the First and Second World Wars. FM radio was invented in 1933, which improved the audio signal of the radio. Nowadays, radio is mostly used to entertain people with music or topic-related discussions. Most radio stations have hourly news updates.

Queen Tube

Queen Elizabeth II launched her own YouTube channel in December 2012 when she used this medium to make her Christmas speech to the people of the United Kingdom.

Viruses

Every month over 6,000 new viruses, which can seriously harm our personal computers, are released.

Social media

Digital social media such as Facebook and Twitter grow daily and are now the world's most powerful media, playing a large part in bringing people together and spreading news. Facebook has over 800 million users. If it were a country, it would be the third largest country in the world after India and China.

Smartphones

Smartphones have made it much easier for people to access digital media while on the move. Most mobile phones are multi-functional now, making it possible not only to phone and text people, but also to take photographs, stay in touch via social media, check and send emails, shop online and play games.

DID YOU KNOW?

Awesome Media Facts

1 WOODEN COMPUTER MOUSE

The first computer mouse was created in 1964 by Doug Engelbert and was made out of a piece of wood.

2 A MASS OF MOBILES

There are more mobile phones on the planet than televisions.

3 WHAT'S YOUR PASSWORD?

Did you know that 123456 is the most common email password?

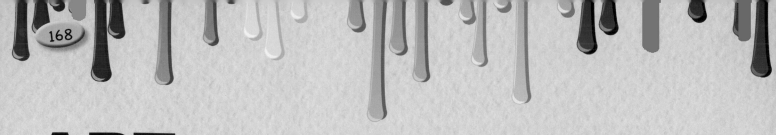

ART

Around 300,000 years ago, the very first artists decorated cave walls with their drawings. Since then people have used art to decorate temples, palaces, landscapes and homes. Art has also been used to honour important people, perhaps with a statue or portrait.

First piece of sculpture

The oldest known sculpture was found in Austria and created 25,000 years ago. It is a sculpture of a pregnant woman with detailed hair, but she has no facial expression.

Pop art

A more recent form of art is called pop art, which started in the mid-1950s in London, and became really popular in the United States in the mid-1960s. Pop art was based on common images or objects, removed from their usual context, being isolated and combined with unrelated material. The most famous pop artist was the American Andy Warhol, who made the famous Marilyn Monroe screenprint.

INTERESTING!

Arty turtles

The Teenage Mutant Ninja Turtles are all named after famous Italian artists from the Renaissance. **Leonardo** (da Vinci) painted the *Mona Lisa* and *The Last Supper*; **Michelangelo** painted the Sistine Chapel in the Vatican; **Donatello** was a famous sculptor; and **Raphael's** paintings are also to be found in the Vatican.

169

Aboriginal art

Australia's Aboriginal peoples created paintings that tell stories about the Dreamtime, which is the time that they believe the Earth was created. They use patterns of dots and lines, different symbols and the colours seen in nature.

AWESOME FACT!

Cold art

Although most art is created to last for many years, usually beyond the artist's lifetime, there is also temporary art. Some artists choose to create ice sculptures, which they then have to photograph for their portfolio before they melt. All over the world festivals are held for the ice artists to show off their skills. In Jukkajärvi, in Sweden, an ice hotel is constructed every winter.

Terracotta army

A bizarre kind of art can be found in China. The first Emperor of China, Qin, built himself a tomb in which he could be guarded by over 8,000 life-sized terracotta soldiers. Each soldier had his own distinct features and weapons, while some even had saddled horses.

Picasso

The early 20th-century Spanish artist Pablo Picasso (1881–1973) started a new art form called Cubism in association with Georges Braque. It is an art form in which the artist looks at a subject, breaks it up into many different shapes, and then repaints it from different angles.

HOMES AROUND THE WORLD

People usually build houses to protect themselves against heat, cold, rain, snow, storms and floods. Houses differ in style all over the world, depending on the weather conditions in that area and the materials available.

Igloos

The Inuit people of northern Canada used to live in houses called igloos made out of blocks of snow. Although most Inuit people now live in tents, huts and houses, igloos are still used by travelling Inuits.

Bedouin tents

All over the world there are people travelling around following herds of sheep or goats. They do not live in the same place all year round. We call these people nomads. The Bedouin are a tribe of nomads living in northern Africa. Their homes are tents woven from camel hair.

Caravans

Travellers and gypsies used to travel around and live in caravans. Roma gypsies have their roots in India before they came to the West, while travellers mainly originate from Ireland. Traveller and gypsy homes are prefabricated in a factory and then taken to the right location on a trailer.

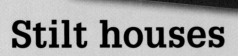

Stilt houses

In Papua New Guinea, the Motuans live in villages built over the sea. The houses are built on stilts to protect them against high tides. The houses last for 20–30 years, depending on the timber used for the stilts. The floors of the houses can be up to 4m (12ft) above the sea. The people of the village help to build each house because they are quite big and can house whole families.

Houseboats

A houseboat is a boat that is especially designed for living in. Most are kept moored to a fixed point on a river or canal, and connected to vital utilities such as water and electricity on land. Houseboats are gaining in popularity as some countries are running out of spare land to build on.

Casablanca

The largest city in Morocco, housing 3.1 million people, is Casablanca. *Casa* means "house" and *blanca* means "white". As you have probably worked out, Casablanca gets its name from all of the white houses in the city. White houses are perfect for keeping cool in the high temperatures in North Africa.

Chalet houses

In the mountains of Switzerland and Austria people live in chalets. These homes are made from wood and have broad roofs, which are designed to withstand heavy snowfall during winter.

Rock homes

In Cappadocia, in eastern Turkey, people have carved homes out of natural cone-shaped rock formations known as "fairy chimneys". These chimneys are caused by erosion over thousands of years.

SEVEN WONDERS OF THE WORLD

When we refer to the Seven Wonders of the World, we are usually talking about the Seven Wonders of the Ancient World. Sadly, only one of these original wonders still survives. There are six groups of new world wonders.

The Ancient Seven Wonders of the World

Of the original Seven Wonders, only the Pyramids of Giza have survived and can still be visited today. People doubt whether the Hanging Gardens of Babylon ever really existed.

Colossus of Rhodes

Hanging Gardens of Babylon

Mausoleum at Halicarnassus

Lighthouse of Alexandria

Pyramids of Giza

Statue of Zeus

Temple of Artemis

Medieval Wonders of the World

As the ancient wonders have all but disappeared, the list of wonders was reviewed and more recent ones included. The medieval wonders are:

Catacombs of Kom el Shoqafa

The Colosseum

Great Wall of China

Hagia Sophia

Leaning Tower of Pisa

Porcelain Tower of Nanjing

Stonehenge

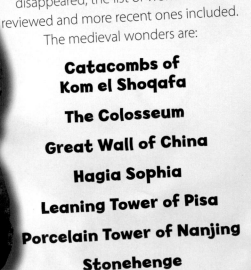

Natural Wonders of the World

Nature has created lots of wonders as well. Although this list is not meant to be definitive, the seven best natural wonders are:

Grand Canyon

Great Barrier Reef

Harbour of Rio de Janeiro

Mount Everest

The Northern Lights

Paricutin Volcano

Victoria Falls

Modern Wonders of the World

Humans have built many great objects over recent years. Here are a few of them:

The Channel Tunnel

CN Tower

Delta Works

Empire State Building

Golden Gate Bridge

Itaipu Dam

Panama Canal

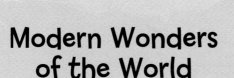

The New Seven Wonders of the World

A project that called for a global vote on what to include in a new list of the Seven Wonders of the World came up with:

Great Wall of China

Potala Palace

Taj Mahal

Roman Colosseum

El Castillo

Moai

Leaning Tower of Pisa

INDEX